T0312055

OTHER PUBLICATIONS FROM THE DRUCKER FOUNDATION

Organizational Leadership Resource

The Drucker Foundation Self-Assessment Tool

The Drucker Foundation Future Series

The Leader of the Future, *Frances Hesselbein, Marshall Goldsmith, Richard Beckhard, Editors*

The Organization of the Future, *Frances Hesselbein, Marshall Goldsmith, Richard Beckhard, Editors*

The Community of the Future, *Frances Hesselbein, Marshall Goldsmith, Richard Beckhard, Richard F. Schubert, Editors*

Wisdom to Action Series

Leading for Innovation, *Frances Hesselbein, Marshall Goldsmith, Iain Somerville, Editors*

Leading Beyond the Walls, *Frances Hesselbein, Marshall Goldsmith, Iain Somerville, Editors*

Leaderbooks

The Collaboration Challenge: How Nonprofits and Businesses Succeed Through Strategic Alliances, *James E. Austin*

Meeting the Collaboration Challenge (workbook and video)

Journal and Related Books

Leader to Leader Journal

Leader to Leader: Enduring Insights on Leadership from the Drucker Foundation's Award-Winning Journal, *Frances Hesselbein, Paul Cohen, Editors*

On High-Performance Organizations, *Frances Hesselbein, Rob Johnston, Editors*

On Leading Change, *Frances Hesselbein, Rob Johnston, Editors*

On Mission and Leadership, *Frances Hesselbein, Rob Johnston, Editors*

Video Training Resources

Excellence in Nonprofit Leadership Video, *featuring Peter F. Drucker, Max De Pree, Frances Hesselbein, and Michele Hunt. Moderated by Richard F. Schubert*

Leading in a Time of Change: What It Will Take to Lead Tomorrow, *a conversation with Peter F. Drucker and Peter M. Senge, introduction by Frances Hesselbein*

Lessons in Leadership Video, *with Peter F. Drucker*

Online Resources

www.drucker.org

On Mission
and Leadership

A DRUCKER FOUNDATION
LEADERBOOK

ABOUT THE DRUCKER FOUNDATION

The Peter F. Drucker Foundation for Nonprofit Management, founded in 1990, takes its name and inspiration from the acknowledged father of modern management. By providing educational opportunities and resources, the foundation furthers its mission "to lead social sector organizations toward excellence in performance." It pursues this mission through the presentation of conferences, video teleconferences, the annual Peter F. Drucker Award for Nonprofit Innovation, and the annual Frances Hesselbein Community Innovation Fellows Program, as well as through the development of management resources, partnerships, and publications.

The Drucker Foundation believes that a healthy society requires three vital sectors: a public sector of effective governments, a private sector of effective businesses, and a social sector of effective community organizations. The mission of the social sector and its organizations is to change lives. It accomplishes this mission by addressing the needs of the spirit, mind, and body of individuals, the community, and society. This sector and its organizations also create a meaningful sphere of effective and responsible citizenship.

In the ten years after its inception, the Drucker Foundation, among other things:

- Presented the Drucker Innovation Award, which each year generates hundreds of applications from local community enterprises; many applicants work in fields in which results are difficult to achieve
- Worked with social sector leaders through the Frances Hesselbein Community Innovation Fellows program
- Held more than twenty conferences in the United States and in countries around the world
- Developed thirteen books: the *Self-Assessment Tool* (revised 1998), for nonprofit organizations; three books in the Drucker Foundation Future Series, *The Leader of the Future* (1996), *The Organization of the Future* (1997), and *The Community of the Future* (1998); *Leader to Leader* (1999); *Leading Beyond the Walls* (1999); *The Collaboration Challenge* (2000); the *Leading in a Time of Change* viewer's workbook and video (2001); *Leading for Innovation* (2002); and *On Mission and Leadership*, *On Leading Change*, *On High-Performance Organizations*, and *On Creativity, Innovation, and Renewal* (all 2002)
- Developed *Leader to Leader*, a quarterly journal for leaders from all three sectors
- Established a Web site (drucker.org) that shares articles on leadership and management and examples of nonprofit innovation with hundreds of thousands of visitors each year

For more information on the Drucker Foundation, contact:

The Peter F. Drucker Foundation for Nonprofit Management
320 Park Avenue, Third Floor, New York, NY 10022-6839 U.S.A.
Telephone: (212) 224-1174 • Fax: (212) 224-2508
E-mail: info@pfdf.org • Web address: www.drucker.org

On Mission and Leadership

A Leader to Leader Guide

Frances Hesselbein
Rob Johnston
Editors

JOSSEY-BASS
A Wiley Company
www.josseybass.com

Published by Jossey-Bass
A Wiley Imprint
989 Market Street, San Francisco, CA 94103-1741   www.josseybass.com

Jossey-Bass books and products are available through most bookstores. To contact Jossey-Bass directly call our Customer Care Department within the U.S. at 800-956-7739, outside the U.S. at 317-572-3986, or fax 317-572-4002.

Jossey-Bass also publishes its books in a variety of electronic formats. Some content that appears in print may not be available in electronic books.

Library of Congress Cataloging-in-Publication Data

On mission and leadership : a leader to leader guide / Frances
Hesselbein and Rob Johnston, editors.
    p. cm.
"Drucker Foundation Leaderbooks."
Includes index.
ISBN 978-0-470-63103-4
1. Corporate culture. 2. Mission statements. 3. Leadership.
I. Hesselbein, Frances. II. Johnston, Rob, date
HD58.7 .O56 2002
658.4'092-dc21   2001007675

FIRST EDITION
HB Printing   10 9 8 7 6 5 4 3

Contents

Introduction

People in the United States and around the world have an enormous hunger for ideas; that's why in 1996 the Drucker Foundation launched *Leader to Leader*, a journal of ideas by leaders for leaders. This hunger among millions of working executives demonstrates their concern for the future and commitment to making a difference.

The incisive thinkers and remarkable leaders who have contributed to the journal and its related books open doors, spark ideas, raise signal flags, and help satisfy that universal hunger. These extraordinary contributors have taught us, among other things, that great leaders do not live isolated from the world; they are engaged with and deeply care about others. They measure their own success by the real-world impact of their work. That people throughout our society and organizations want to contribute to a better world has been a major premise of *Leader to Leader*.

We learned, too, that astonishing things happen when you give intelligent, effective people a free hand. Never have we approached our authors with an assigned topic or reviewed their work before an advisory board or peer review; when you're working with the best in the world, you don't do that. Rather, we simply asked, "What's on your mind? What issues will most affect leaders, organizations, or communities in the coming years?" From that unfettered process, several coherent themes emerged with astonishing clarity. They are evident in the four volumes of the Leader to Leader Guides. This volume, *On Mission and Leadership*, explores the essential role that mission plays in defining and supporting leadership. The effective organization is built around mission—the reason for being—and effective leaders mobilize around and communicate mission at all times. Also those leaders live and demonstrate the values and character that the organization needs to succeed. They build community within the organization and the organization's role in the community outside.

The other volumes in this series are *On Leading Change*, which explores the challenges of bringing organizations through transformation; *On High-Performance Organizations*, which explores getting the most from the people and other resources of each organization; and *On Creativity, Innovation, and Renewal*, which explores how leaders can keep an organization changing with a focus on building the future.

We gathered the wisdom of our contributors so that our readers could find insight and inspiration to make a difference in their organizations and their communities. We hope our collection will help you to lead, to inspire a change, to strengthen your performance, or to spark and sustain a renewal. We wish you the best as you apply these lessons to the work you do and the people you touch.

February 2002   Frances Hesselbein
                                             Easton, Pennsylvania

                                             Rob Johnston
                                             New York, New York

About the Editors

Frances Hesselbein is chairman of the board of governors of the Peter F. Drucker Foundation for Nonprofit Management and is the former chief executive of the Girl Scouts of the U.S.A. She is a member of the boards of other organizations and corporations and is the lead editor of the Drucker Foundation's best-selling books, including *The Leader of the Future, The Organization of the Future, The Community of the Future, Leading Beyond the Walls,* and *Leader to Leader,* published by Jossey-Bass. She also serves as editor in chief of the journal *Leader to Leader.* She speaks on leadership and management to audiences around the world in the private, nonprofit, and governmental sectors. She has received fifteen honorary doctorates and was awarded the Presidential Medal of Freedom in 1998.

Rob Johnston is president and CEO of the Peter F. Drucker Foundation for Nonprofit Management. He has served the Drucker Foundation since 1991 and was appointed president effective March 2001. At the foundation he has led program development, the Drucker Innovation Award program, publication development, and teleconference and conference development.

He was executive producer for *Leading in a Time of Change*, a 2001 video featuring Peter F. Drucker and Peter M. Senge, and for *The Nonprofit Leader of the Future*, the foundation's 1997 video teleconference broadcast to 10,000 leaders across the United States. He leads the editorial development of the foundation's Web site (drucker.org) and is a senior editor for *Leader to Leader*. Johnston earned a B.A. degree in the history of art from Yale and an M.B.A. degree from Stanford. He contributed a chapter to *Enterprising Nonprofits* (John Wiley & Sons, 2001).

On Mission and Leadership

**A DRUCKER FOUNDATION
LEADERBOOK**

1

Speaking a Common Language

Frances Hesselbein

As today's leaders move among business, nonprofit, and government sectors and across countries, they are learning to speak a common language. This is a language of organizational vision, values, and mission, of the strategies based on them, and of serving the needs of the customer, no matter what the organization's goal, product, or service is.

Today leaders speak a common language. It is understood across the borders that once separated business, nonprofits, and government and moves just as easily across cultures, countries, and continents. It is a global language of *mission, strategy,* and *customer,* as readily understood by leaders in Beijing as in Boston.

To today's business, government, and nonprofit leaders of change, the principles of leadership are basic, generic to all organizations, and universal in their reach and relevance.

That is the message I delivered in October 2000 in a series of seminars in China. At the invitation of the Bright China Management Institute, a team of four thought leaders with the Drucker Foundation met with more than 2000 business, government, and emerging social sector leaders. For seven days in three cities we talked about managing for the mission—the need for leaders to hold before their people why they do what they do, their reason for being. As we talked with our Chinese colleagues, we used the same language to describe the power of mission that we use when we work with the Salvation Army, the U.S. Army, Texaco, or the American Federation of Arts. Vision. Mission. Goals. The actual words are different in every language, but the power of those words is universal. And with a common language, people in every sector, in every culture, can have dialogues of great meaning. This has not always been the case.

Ten years ago, when the Drucker Foundation was founded, some in the social sector questioned whether *customer* could be used to describe their clients, patients, service recipients, or members. But slowly the word became part of a management vocabulary that enabled social sector leaders to communicate without translation.

It was clear that common characteristics demanded common terms—a common glossary. The powerful management books by Peter F. Drucker, Charles Handy, Peter Senge, Regina Herzlinger, and James Austin spoke to no single sector—they belonged to all three. Jim Collins and Jerry Porras's *Built to Last* made as much sense to the Girl Scouts as to General Motors—this at the same time that the *Army Leadership Field Manual* is as relevant to a newly commissioned lieutenant, a noncommissioned officer, or a civilian employee as to a colonel.

Throughout the three sectors, a marvelous sense of inclusion and collaboration permeates our organizations, our enterprises. Our common leadership language unleashes new alliances, new partnerships, new understanding as organizations in all three sectors move beyond the walls of the old and toward a new realization of the common good.

For instance, Investment in America, a forum of The Conference Board, the U.S. Army, and the Drucker Foundation, supports the army's Partnership for Youth Success, through which 200 corporations promise good jobs to young men and women when they complete their military service. No need for translation in this partnership. And the Texaco Management Institute delivers world-class management training to leaders of advocacy and other nonprofit groups. For them, managing for the mission, for innovation, for diversity resonates in both the corporation and the community.

The rapid proliferation of college and university nonprofit-management programs is also building a common vocabulary for change, partnership, and community. In 1998, there were 180 colleges and universities with courses in nonprofit management, up from just 17 in 1990. Here again, listening to the customer has become the common focus—the common language.

Demographics-driven is as relevant to a college as to an e-commerce start-up, and innovation is a universal imperative. When we cling to our insider vocabulary, we end up talking to ourselves. Today even *marketing*—once a suspect word in some corners of the public and nonprofit sectors—has become an essential discipline, with a new understanding that it is about serving the needs of customers.

The nuances of the new language allow for true dialogue. No longer do we settle for the didactic pronouncement, "Nonprofits have to be managed like businesses." Today we respond, "No, nonprofits must manage in a businesslike way." Similar words, different meanings, new understanding.

Values-based is as essential for the American Red Cross as for American Express. At one time there was little movement across the sectors—corporate executives climbed the corporate ladder; nonprofit executives moved, perhaps, to other nonprofits; and government leaders found their way to and from the other sectors. Today there is a flow of corporate and government executives to nonprofit leadership roles—James Hayes from *Fortune* magazine to Junior Achievement, Dr. Bernadine Healy from the National Institutes of Health to the American Red Cross, Admiral Marsha Evans from the U.S. Navy to the Girl Scouts of the U.S.A. Each move underscores the fluidity of leadership among all sectors, and each leader speaks the more inclusive, nonhierarchical language of the future. There is no up-down, top-bottom, superior-subordinate language for the newly mobile, newly agile, emerging leadership corps. These leaders are as at ease in the boardroom as in the classroom.

I travel frequently, spending one-third of my time with corporations, one-third with social sector nonprofits, and one-third with colleges and universities. As I travel from Australia to Denmark to Mexico to China to Peru to Poland—and in the United States—wherever I find an airport and an audience I use the same philosophy and choose the same words. Both are fundamental and generic. The examples and applications may change, but the message is circular and universal.

There is wonderment in the ease with which our leaders transcend the old barriers, breach the old walls, and share a new appreciation of the differences that can enrich our lives. For such leaders, language is more than a tool, a skill, or a simple vehicle for communication. It is the thread that binds us together, creates new understanding, leads us to new action, and then strengthens and builds communities. It is men and women speaking the language of inclusion, appreciation, and wholeness who sustain the democracy.

Frances Hesselbein is editor in chief of *Leader to Leader,* chairman of the board of governors of the Drucker Foundation, and former chief executive of the Girl Scouts of the U.S.A.

2

The Leadership Advantage

Warren Bennis

Intellectual capital is an organization's primary asset. Knowledge workers seek meaning and purpose in their work, a climate of trust and optimism, and results. To retain and motivate knowledge workers, leaders need more than technical competence, strategic thinking, and "people" skills; they need the ability to identify and cultivate talent, and they need good judgment and character.

Never has the subject of leadership been of greater interest to managers, or to management writers. Richard Donkins, writing in the *Financial Times*, describes "a fixation bordering on obsession [with] the qualities needed for corporate leadership." It is, he adds, a "contagious" obsession, spreading in scope and intensity throughout our society, and suggesting that Americans have lost their way.

If it is an obsession, it is a useful one for any organization concerned about the future—but I understand the source of the frustration Donkins and others display. For all the ink the subject gets in scholarly, business, and popular journals, leadership remains an elusive concept.

However, whether or not leadership is well understood, its impact on the bottom line is dramatic, according to a study by Andersen Consulting's Institute for Strategic Change: the stock price of companies perceived as being well led grew 900 percent over a 10-year period, compared to just 74 percent growth in companies perceived to lack good leadership. And *Fortune*, in its 1998 roundup of America's most admired companies, identifies the common denominator of exemplary organizations. "The truth is that no one factor makes a company admirable," wrote Thomas Stewart, "but if you were forced to pick the one that makes the most difference, you'd pick leadership. In Warren Buffet's phrase, 'People are voting for the artist and not the painting.'"

Generating Intellectual Capital

My own observations of organizations and leadership lead me to two conclusions about what it will take to survive in the tumultuous years ahead: (1) The key to future competitive advantage will be the organization's capacity to create the social architecture capable of generating intellectual capital, and (2) leadership is the key to realizing the full potential of intellectual capital.

Percy Barnevik, former chairman of ABB and one of Europe's most celebrated business leaders, says that "organizations ensure that [people] use only 5 to 10 percent of their abilities at work. Outside of work they engage the other 90 to 95 percent." The challenge for leaders, he adds, is "to learn how to recognize and employ that untapped ability." His assessment is supported by data on both sides of the Atlantic. Nearly two-thirds of companies surveyed by Kepner-Tregoe say they don't use more than half their employees' brainpower. And employees themselves are even less optimistic; only 16 percent said they use more than half their talents at work, according to a recent U.K. survey.

On the other hand, huge benefits accrue to organizations that, as Barnevik urges, learn to employ their collective brainpower, know-how, ideas, and innovation. A study of 3,200 U.S. companies, conducted by Robert Zemsky and Susan Shaman of the University of Pennsylvania, showed that a 10 percent increase in spending for workforce training and development leads to an 8.5 percent increase in productivity; a similar increase in capital expenditures leads to just a 3.8 percent increase in productivity.

Such findings explain why the long-time CEO of General Electric, Jack Welch, says he had only three jobs as CEO: selecting the right people, allocating capital resources, and spreading ideas quickly. Welch typically asked the hundreds of GE managers he talked with not only about their ideas but who they'd shared their ideas with, and who else had adopted them.

It is no accident that both Welch and Barnevik, two of the world's most accomplished business leaders, see their roles in similar terms. In a knowledge economy, leaders cannot command employees to work harder, smarter, or faster. Knowledge workers, if they are earning their pay, know more about their work than the CEO does, and are in great demand. Without leaders who can attract and retain talent, manage knowledge, and unblock people's capacity to adapt and innovate, an organization's future is in jeopardy.

Qualities of a Leader

Though Donkins implies that our search for the qualities of leadership is futile, research points to seven attributes essential to leadership. Taken together they provide a framework for leading knowledge workers:

Technical competence: business literacy and grasp of one's field

Conceptual skill: a facility for abstract or strategic thinking

Track record: a history of achieving results

People skills: an ability to communicate, motivate, and delegate

Taste: an ability to identify and cultivate talent

Judgment: making difficult decisions in a short time frame with imperfect data

Character: the qualities that define who we are

Senior executives seldom lack the first three attributes; rarely do they fail because of technical or conceptual incompetence, nor do they reach high levels of responsibility without having a strong track record. All these skills are important, but in tomorrow's world exemplary leaders will be distinguished by their mastery of the softer side: people skills, taste, judgment, and, above all, character.

Character is the key to leadership—an observation confirmed by most people's personal experience, as it is in my 15 years of work with more than 150 leaders and in the other studies I've encountered. Research at Harvard University indicates that 85 percent of a leader's performance depends on personal character. Likewise, the work of Daniel Goleman makes clear that leadership success or failure is usually due to "qualities of the heart" (see "The Emotional Intelligence of Leaders," this volume). Although character is less quantifiable than other aspects of leadership, there are many ways to take the measure of an individual (see "The Anatomy of Character").

Demands of Followers

Power in the knowledge economy resides more with knowledge workers than with owners or managers. Serving the needs of those workers is a new leadership imperative. Research shows not only the characteristics of effective leaders but also the expectations that followers have of their leaders. Whether in a corporation, a Scout troop, a public agency, or an entire nation, constituents seek four things: meaning or direction, trust in and from the leader, a sense of hope and optimism, and results. To serve these constituent needs—and ultimately to unleash an organization's intellectual capital—leaders can foster four supporting conditions, which in turn can create four respective outcomes (see table).

To satisfy followers' needs and achieve positive outcomes,
leaders must provide four things.

In Service of Constituent Needs for:	Leaders Provide:	To Help Create:
Meaning and direction	Sense of purpose	Goals and objectives
Trust	Authentic relationships	Reliability and consistency
Hope and optimism	"Hardiness" (confidence that things will work out)	Energy and commitment
Results	Bias toward action, risk, curiosity, and courage	Confidence and creativity

Exemplary Leadership

The Anatomy of Character

There are many definitions of character, but for exemplary leaders character goes beyond ethical behavior (although that is essential). The word itself comes from the Greek for *engraved* or *inscribed*. For the leaders I have studied, character has to do with who we are, with how we organize our experience. The great psychologist William James described it as "the particular mental or moral attitude [that makes one feel] most deeply and intensively active and alive . . . a voice inside which speaks and says, 'This is the real me.'" Effective leaders—and effective people—know that voice well. They understand that there is no difference between becoming an effective leader and becoming a fully integrated human being.

Many aspects of character—such as our degree of energy or our cognitive skill—are probably determined at birth; others are influenced by our family life, our birth order, our relationships with parents, teachers, and friends. Yet character develops throughout life, including work life. Leaders can help others become more aware of their innate capacities. For example, by examining the kinds of decisions they make and don't make, senior executives and those they manage can develop their own character and cultivate new leadership throughout the organization.

For executive leaders, character is framed by drive, competence, and integrity. Most senior executives have the drive and competence necessary to lead. But too often organizations elevate people who lack the moral compass. I call them "destructive achievers." They are seldom evil people, but by using resources for no higher purpose than achievement of their own goals, they often diminish the enterprise. Such leaders seldom last, for the simple reason that without all three ingredients—drive, competence, and moral compass—it is difficult to engage others and sustain meaningful results.

• *Providing purpose.* Effective leaders bring passion, perspective, and significance to the process of defining organizational purpose.

Every effective leader I've known is passionate about what he
or she is doing. The time and energy devoted to work demand a
commitment and conviction bordering on love. Michael Eisner,
chairman of the Walt Disney Company, defines that quality as a
strong point of view, or in Hollywood parlance, POV. In his company, he says, it is unfailingly the person with conviction who
wins the day. "Around here," adds Eisner (we're talking about
Hollywood, remember), POV is worth at least 80 IQ points."

One starts with passion; perspective is harder to come by—
but is essential in a world of rapid change. For most people in
organizations, the question is not only what happens next, but
what happens *after* what happens next. As hockey great Wayne
Gretzky explains, "It ain't where the puck is, it's where the
puck will be." One Fortune 500 CEO puts it differently: "If
you're not confused, you don't know what's going on." Because
the fog of reality is so pervasive, constituents want not just a
vision of where we're heading but also where they've been and
where they are now. People want leaders to provide context.

Finally, knowledge workers—the best of whom have significant choice in the place and terms of their employment—want
a sense of significance.

What is the meaning of our work?

What difference or larger contribution does it make
to others?

How do we measure success?

And what are the positive outcomes of that success?

By making time for such reflection, leaders build support for organizational goals and objectives.

• *Generating and sustaining trust.* Since 1985, 20 percent of the American workforce has been laid off at least once. In a time when the new social contract makes the ties between organizations and their knowledge workers tenuous, trust becomes the emotional glue that can bond people to an organization.

These are the factors that generate trust—at work or in a partnership, a marriage, or a friendship: competence, constancy, caring, candor, congruity.

What I call congruity—or authenticity, feeling comfortable with oneself—is a further reflection of character. It is at the heart of any honest relationship. But congruity goes beyond simply knowing yourself; it is being consistent, presenting the same face at work as at home.

Candor is perhaps the most important component of trust. When we are truthful about our shortcomings or acknowledge that we do not have all the answers, we earn the understanding and respect of others.

Exemplary leaders create a climate of candor throughout their organizations. They remove the organizational barriers—and the fear—that cause people to keep bad news from the boss. They understand that those closest to customers usually have the solutions but can do little unless a climate of candor allows problems to be discussed. Especially during times of change, exemplary leaders share information about what's going on in the organization, the industry, and the world. They treat candor as one measure of personal and organizational performance, which can be gauged through employees' response to such statements as, "My organization encourages people to take the time to communicate openly, even about difficult questions." Or, "There is little fear of speaking openly about important issues."

Without candor there can be no trust. And by building trust, leaders help create the reliability and consistency customers demand.

- *Fostering hope.* Exemplary leaders seem to expect success; they always anticipate positive outcomes. The glass for them is not simply full but brimming.

Hope combines the determination to achieve one's goals with the ability to generate the means to do so. Hopeful people describe themselves with such statements as

I can think of ways to get out of a jam.

I energetically pursue my goals.

My experience has prepared me well for the future.

There are ways around any problem.

One example of a hopeful leader is former Intel Chairman Andrew Grove, who told me 15 years ago that he grew up with a "Nobel complex." He emigrated from Hungary speaking little English, with no money, but his parents imbued in him a sense that he would succeed in whatever he attempted. If he went into science, he told me, he felt he could win the Nobel Prize. That psychological hardiness, the sense that things generally work out well, creates tremendous confidence in oneself and in those around one. And that kind of confidence influences others. It builds energy and commitment, and that in turn influences outcomes. In short, every exemplary leader that I have met has what seems to be an unwarranted degree of optimism—and that helps generate the energy and commitment necessary to achieve results.

- *Getting results.* As leaders we can provide meaning, build trust, and foster hope, but all of that counts for little unless an organization produces results.

Most leaders coming into a new position or facing a moment of truth are afforded some time and resources to deliver. That is what makes a collective sense of purpose, trust, and hope so important—they can carry people through what they know will be a difficult time. But these assets will dissipate if leaders do not get results. And of course we deliver results only by taking action. That does not mean that every action will be successful. But, as Gretzky reminds us, "You miss 100 percent of the shots you don't take." Exemplary leaders never forget that they must ultimately take their best shots—and create a climate that tolerates missed shots yet demands that everyone continue to take them. Moving from talk to action is imperative, but, especially in the times we live in, it requires commitment, enterprise, curiosity—and courage. It requires leadership.

Results-oriented leaders see themselves as catalysts. They expect to achieve a great deal, but know that they can do little without the efforts of others. They bring the zeal, resourcefulness, risk-tolerance—and discipline—of the entrepreneur to every effort of the organization. Nothing less will break through the noise, clutter, and competitive pressure of today's marketplace.

To be sure, we are paying unprecedented attention to the subject of leadership. We are also seeing the importance of intellectual capital to strategy, organizational design, leadership development, employee retention, and virtually every business practice that matters. Organizations that don't take such issues seriously, or that fail to make the connection between leadership and the quality of their intellectual capital, will probably not be in the phone book in 2002.

One CEO says, "We are making the topic of leadership an issue we have powerful conversations about. We encourage people to talk about it. We reward coaches. We want people to develop ways of getting feedback." They do so not as an exercise but as a way to compete. Exemplary leaders believe they have a responsibility to extend people's growth and to create an environment where people constantly learn. Those are the surest ways to generate intellectual capital and to use that capital to create new value. In the next century, that will be every leader's ultimate task.

Warren Bennis is distinguished professor of business administration and founding chairman of the Leadership Institute at the University of Southern California's Marshall School of Business. He has advised 4 U.S. presidents and more than 150 CEOs and is author or coauthor of more than 20 books on leadership, change, and management, including *Organizing Genius* and his most recent, *Co-Leaders*.

3

Leader as Social Advocate: Building the Business by Building Community

An Interview with Anita Roddick

In this interview, Anita Roddick states that nonprofits are becoming more businesslike and businesses are developing social values and seeking to contribute to the community. Believing that principles and profits are not in conflict, she proposes new ways to measure success, such as engaging employees' hearts and customer loyalty through meaningful accomplishment, standing for something, and operating as multi-local rather than multinational.

A key skill of leadership is "finding one's voice"—articulating the ideas, values, passions, and aspirations that can inspire commitment. One of the clearest, sometimes loudest, voices in corporate leadership is Anita Roddick, founder of The Body Shop International.

Since opening her first skin-care shop in 1976 she has built one of the world's most recognized retail brands and created a niche for naturally based products. Recognized for its independently audited social and environmental practices, the company sources many of its ingredients directly from producers in developing countries, creating sustainable local economies. It has campaigned for human rights, fought the animal testing of cosmetics, and contributed money and personnel to nongovernmental organizations in Kosovo, Romania, Brazil, and elsewhere. Roddick spoke with *Leader to Leader* about the role of the business leader as social advocate.

Leader to Leader: The mission of The Body Shop is, in part, the pursuit of social and environmental change. You seem to make almost no distinction between a business and a social institution. Is that a realistic model for others?

Anita Roddick: Yes, it is. What's interesting is that nonprofit organizations are having to act in a much more appropriate business way—to be more focused, more strategic. And many businesses are adopting almost a nonprofit agenda, in terms of defining their mission. They are looking at not just the enhancement of profits but at how the business is perceived in the local community.

The big question that none of us in business ever want to ask ourselves—because I think we'd probably all close down—is, does the growth of the business presuppose the destruction of the planet? Is the continuing need for growth—the way we're measured in terms of success—a philosophy that will destroy the environment? Does our financial growth automatically mean that we will alienate humanity in every way?

No, that doesn't need to happen, but growth in itself is a real problem. We don't have a culture that says, "What about growth of the human spirit rather than the growth of profits?"

And how to redefine profits? The two agendas, business and social, can work together. There are a lot of examples of how. But the bigger question of growth is a hard one, because anyone who has spent a lot of time traveling and seeing the actions of businesses around the world has a real disquiet about the drive for endless growth.

L2L: You're saying business leaders should look beyond the narrow confines of the business itself. Isn't that asking them to do something that they were not hired to do?

AR: You see, the narrow confines are getting narrower and narrower. When you see the huge growth of international money flows—the way billions of dollars can cross borders via computer with no restrictions and certainly no bloody taxes—the notion of profit is there for relatively few people. Mostly it doesn't go down into the community or the broad base of employees.

I'm asking businesses to seriously look at some old business practitioners—like the Quakers, who were incredibly successful businesspeople, cared about their community, never paid themselves more than they needed to, and saw business as a community of peoples and the protection of those peoples. They measured success in a different way. I think there's a resurgence of that way of thinking as an antidote for the belief that profits are everything.

L2L: Well, how do you measure success?

AR: People are always thinking in business there's only one measurement, which is financial. What about measuring success by the joy in the workplace? Or by meeting environmental and social standards? These measures are out there: people are working on them. But most business leaders are afraid to consider them.

My measure of success is how influential and inspirational I can be, how continually progressive I manage to be. But at the same time, I feel there is a real tyranny in measurements. You see that so clearly in business. It's no longer about honorable trade, the buying and selling of a product. Instead it's become a financial science, and its language is necessarily confining. So when you challenge the language of business—by bringing in other ways to measure success, for example—you're challenging the very foundation of business. It drives economists nuts.

L2L: Still, business leaders are accountable for financial performance. What are the benefits to the business of social engagement?

AR: It's to do with the development of the human spirit. When anything comes from the heart—any energy, any action—it comes with a passion that is unstoppable. My staff does not go home dreaming of moisture creams. They go home absolutely riveted when they come back from a project in Bosnia or Kosovo. The experience has changed their values. When you have a process of education that goes on in a company—not educating to sell but a bigger education—people don't want to leave you.

There's also something to providing a safe area where you can practice things that you're not taught at school: advocacy, activism. There's nothing more joyous in retailing—which is a freaking dull industry, mostly populated by women, by the way—than to engage in the community, to do volunteerism on company time. So where's the benefit? There's a passion that persuades, that binds both customers and employees to you, that sparks innovation. And in our case, in the business of skin and hair care, we don't advertise, but we garner an enormous amount of attention on some of our actions, whether liked or not liked.

We're not an anonymous company because we stand for something—and we are claiming a territory where the competition won't follow.

L2L: Is part of your job to create an identity for yourself and your organization?

AR: We never sat down and said, "How can we be different?" A social commitment comes out of a belief in yourself, because as an entrepreneur what you're doing is putting out a thumbprint of who you are. Being the rabble-rouser that I am, I want my thumbprint on the canvas of The Body Shop. But at the same time, the values I hold on to go far beyond the 'me.'

The leader has to have a moral agenda. If the leader is only saying we want to be the biggest or the most profitable company in the world, forget it. When you do that, there's no leadership. There's nothing more to aspire to. But if your aspirations come from the values of your culture or church or temple or mosque, you have something beyond your own livelihood creation. You're coming to work not as a nine-to-five sort of death but a nine-to-five sort of living. Leaders have to lay out a concept and see what their amazing group of people can do. It's not just about compassion, it's about meaningful accomplishment.

L2L: You lead both within the organization and in the community. Is there a difference? How do you bridge the two?

AR: In the organization, it doesn't have to be any more complicated than motivation. And to do that, you have to live and breathe with the troops, not just the top guys. My greatest hope in the organization is to reach a level where I can absolutely inspire young people, mostly female, to have a voice. Their voice is trained to be timid. From day one, young girls in our society are never told they're remarkable. The minute they can open their eyes they've got ads telling them to get a facelift or diet. My role is helping them to reclaim their freedom to say no, to be heard, to make sure that in anything they do—whether it's in their relationships, in love, in work and the community—they have the right to be heard. They give away their power so often. I try to make the connection between the work of the organization and the larger community.

L2L: Recently your business has been under pressure—with lower profits and lower sales in established stores. Do you lead differently during tough times? How do you establish priorities within the organization, or between the business and the community, when the business is tested?

AR: We've had real dilemmas in the past three years because we've been going through the difficult and necessary process of completely restructuring the business. There was so much media misinterpretation—actually, we made a profit of £27 million ($40 million) in 1999!

But it was never our commitment to social responsibility that was a cause of a decline in the price/earnings ratio. Principles and profits are not in conflict, and if profits dip, it's because you're not running your business smartly enough, or your products don't hold the same fascination, or you've got a distribution system that's strangling you.

It all comes down to communication. We knew we had to regionalize our operation; it's ludicrous to manufacture everything from one site in the United Kingdom. We want to protect workers, especially blue-collar workers. But for the first time we had to face redundancies. The process had to be part of who we are. So we talked to everybody in the organization. Everybody knew what was happening. For people who could not con-tinue with the organization, or who didn't want to, we offered retraining packages to the entire family—it might have been a parent or spouse who wanted to take job training. We set up an Entrepreneur's Club; we provided money to seed people's own ventures, to work with the community, or to come back as a consultant to the company. And we worked with everybody in the community—health-care workers, social workers, police, psychologists—so everyone understood our process.

That we haven't been deflected even more seriously in our business is an amazement to me. What has kept us going from all the regions of the world where we're having to reorganize is our common set of values—our human rights campaigning, our social justice. That's the glue that has kept us together.

L2L: How do you communicate with over 5,000 employees in over 1,700 stores around the world, and with all those you want to reach outside the company?

AR: I'm very good on communications. Communication is a delivery system. I can take any vehicle—Internet, newsletter, whatever—and address whatever issue is important. We have a series of booklets coming out of my office called *Full Voice*, which talks about our community trade or the unattainable ideals pro-moted by the cosmetics industry. I've written a weekly column for the *Independent on Sunday*, a national newspaper in the UK. I travel consistently to the shops—yesterday I was in five. We've used audiocassettes, monthly videos. It's all about the champi-oning of products and the values of the company.

L2L: The Body Shop is in name and in fact an international organization operating in 48 countries. But you take a dim view of multinational businesses. How are you different?

AR: I take a really dim view, yes. The difference is, we are not multinational, we are multi-local. Multi-local is when people, families or couples, set up their own entrepreneurial business. They're rooted in the community, and we end up wholesaling to them. There's no central power within The Body Shop International. There may be moral influence but there's no power, there's no lobbying behind the scenes with the World Trade Organization.

The multinational corporations are really the owners of the planet. They control government behavior, they impose their obsession with deregulation, their obsession with trading within just the top G-7 countries. They are probably the biggest human rights abusers—in terms of employment practices, their collusion with the armies in Burma or Nigeria, the list is endless. One of the great mysteries to me is why the media haven't glommed onto these abuses. Businesses need to be accountable, and when necessary, penalized. We all have to clean up our mess. And we have to be honest, transparent in our business practices. That's why it's exciting to see the growth of the vigilante consumer groups—people who are not targeting governments but targeting and boycotting and pressuring corporations. Nothing's going to happen unless there's consumer outrage. And that is rooted in education.

L2L: How do you keep the issues that are important to you relevant to others in the organization, and to customers?

AR: It's hard to get The Body Shop as excited as I am by a lot of these things. And new people come in and they're so respectful of what I've achieved. But you know something? They don't quite get it. It's a problem of language—they talk about consumers and I talk about customers; they talk about the brand and I talk about The Body Shop. I'm consistently trying to find more humane or more intimate language.

Is this what consumers want? I don't care a whit what the consumers want. You find what is right and then you take it and shape it in such a wonderful way that people will rally to it. For me, the things I always loved were product development, style, image—in a way, marketing, but we never had a marketing department for 17 years. We won lots of awards for marketing but we never really knew what it was. Now we have young kids running product development. The guardians at the gateposts have changed. But I can influence morally, I can influence by design. And I can influence by passion.

L2L: What are you doing to develop that next generation of leaders within the company?

AR: One of the worst things is what I've not done. I'm so protective of the stuff I've done in the past, like going out to pre-industrial communities and coming back with product ideas, that I should be mentoring others to do that. But I have this profound belief that it's got to come from the heart. You've got to have the will to create, got to have a real love of curiosity. I tend to measure our employees by how many questions they ask. I go to every shop and ask, "Where are you from, where are your parents from?"

Earlier today a wonderful, charming woman from Nicaragua served me at my hotel. I went to the manager and said, "I'm going to tell you something. You've got the most wonderful employees." She looked at me like I'd just dropped down from another planet because she expected to be harangued. There's such a poverty of praise in organizations. So another aspect of leadership is the praise, if it's meaningful. In other words, we perpetuate our vision and values by living them.

L2L: You speak about "managing by falling apart at the seams." What does that mean?

AR: Organizations are consistently falling apart at the seams—emotionally and every other way. There are so many crises of management, of everyday life, of change. Every business has words for it, and they are always economic words. Try bringing in words like "grace" and "awe" and "wonderment"—poetic words that could describe the actions of people in a company. Maybe it's the optimism of the entrepreneur or the rebel, but leaders find a seam of meaning. Sometimes that seam is lost in the maelstrom of organizational and personal change; the creative organization should never be a comfortable place anyway. It's a matter of managing that tension and remaining hopeful and creative.

L2L: What would you like to leave as your legacy?

AR: I hope that when the epitaphs are being written, they will say that this was one of the first companies to try to change the language and the behavior of business, that brought a social engagement to everything it did, and shouted this from the rooftops.

If you're passionate about certain things—as I am—you speak out. There's a great quote: "If I'd wanted to be quiet I would have opened a library." So I want to be heard. George Bernard Shaw, when he talked about the nature of his life, said it was like holding onto a flame, seeing how strong that flame can burn, and then passing it on. That was a wonderful message for me.

Anita Roddick is founder and co-chair of The Body Shop International. With more than 1,700 stores in 48 countries, the company reported 1999 sales of more than $900 million (£606 million). Roddick has won numerous business, leadership, and philanthropic awards including the Order of the British Empire. She is author of *Body and Soul* and *Business as Usual*.

4

The Emotional Intelligence of Leaders

Daniel Goleman

Emotional intelligence is more important to successful leadership than IQ or technical expertise. Emotional intelligence includes self-awareness and the abilities to manage one's emotions and impulses, motivate others, show empathy, and stay connected. Successful leaders select for and reward employees based on their EI. They also make efforts to develop employees' emotional intelligence in order to enhance decision making, the ability to take the long-range view, and a range of other productive behaviors.

Some years ago my wife and I were driving out of Manhattan on a wet winter afternoon. We were crawling in bumper-to-bumper traffic up the West Side Highway, when I was amazed to see a man in a wheelchair between the lanes of traffic, begging. I was so shocked and touched by his plight I automatically reached into my pocket as my car went by and dropped a $5 bill into his cup. Then out of the corner of my eye I saw a gust of wind catch the bill and drop it on the roadway. I watched a drama unfold in my rearview mirror: the man couldn't bend down to get the money; he had no legs. To my amazement, a passenger in the car behind me got out of the back door, walked along with the car so as not to hold up traffic, picked up the bill, put it in the cup, got back in the car, and rode away.

That person was a true leader: he recognized a human problem and stepped in to create a solution. He showed both the qualities of leadership and the qualities of the heart, which I believe are largely the same. The competencies that distinguish someone as a human being also distinguish him or her as a leader. People in leadership roles seldom lack credentials. Yet we all know—and probably have worked for—individuals with obvious intelligence, ambition, and skill who were incompetent in the human arena.

Clearly there's a difference between rational and emotional intelligence. Both are essential to success, but only the former is in abundant evidence in organizational leadership. There is little variation in IQ among most people in leadership positions; in technical or professional arenas, people need an IQ of 115 or 120 to get into their field. However, there is huge variation in their emotional capability, which, unlike innate intelligence, can be consciously developed. Thus, in a realm in which, to paraphrase Garrison Keillor, all leaders are above average, being at the top of one's emotional game confers great benefits.

Studies of outstanding performers in hundreds of organizations show that about two-thirds of the abilities that set apart star performers from the rest are based on emotional intelligence; only one-third of the skills that matter relate to raw intelligence and technical expertise. In fact, one study of the senior executives of 52 global organizations found that only about 10 percent of the skills that distinguish these leaders are purely intellectual in nature. And we know anecdotally that high achievers in many organizations are denied senior leadership positions because they fail to inspire, motivate, or respect others—even if a few emotionally challenged cases do make it to the top.

The Anatomy of Emotions

Our emotions are hardwired into our being. The very architecture of the brain gives feelings priority over thought. The human brain evolved from the bottom up: the brain stem, at the base of the skull, controls involuntary functions like heart rate and reflexes. The limbic system, around and above the brain stem, developed later and handles our emotions. The cortex and neocortex, which evolved long after the limbic system, are the centers for complex thinking.

A structure in the limbic system called the *amygdala* ("almond" in Greek) stores all emotional memory—everything in life that made us angry, sad, or happy. The amygdala, in addition to preceding the cortex by thousands of generations, occupies a privileged position in the brain. It has a direct connection to the thalamus, which processes all incoming sensory information. In effect, we scan everything that happens to us moment to moment through our emotional memories to see if it resembles anything that made us angry, sad, or happy in the past. If the emotional brain doesn't like what it is seeing, it will declare an emotional emergency, an amygdala hijack. You have a sudden, intense emotional reaction, and when it's over you think, "I wish I hadn't said that." It has happened to all of us. Fortunately, the amygdala impulse, "This guy is making me so mad I'd like to slug him," is sent to the prefrontal cortex, which brings together information from all parts of the brain, and adds, "Oh, but this is my boss." So you think, "OK, I will not slug him; I'll smile and change the subject."

In short, we cannot extricate thought from emotion except in the most purely abstract domains. We can be effective only when the two systems—our emotional brain and our thinking brain—work together. That working relationship, which encompasses most of what we do in life, is the essence of emotional intelligence. There are five dimensions of emotional intelligence, each of which describes a basic human ability that is also the foundation for specific capabilities of leadership.

1. *Self-awareness.* We seldom pay attention to what we feel. A stream of moods runs in parallel to our stream of thoughts, but we most often are lost in thought. We're thinking about the next thing to do, planning this, remembering that, grappling with a decision. But when we face a turning point in life—Should I trust this deal? Should I leave this job? Should I marry this person?— we ignore the background murmur of moods at our own peril.

The reason, again, is biological. The brain is not programmed to give a neat accounting of the 25 life experiences that would provide a bottom-line basis for our decision. Rather, according to neurologist Antonio Damasio, the amygdala calculates the emotional bottom line from our relevant life experience and gives us an answer through a gut feeling—literally. The neurotransmitter system for this response runs into the gastrointestinal tract and tells you viscerally, "This doesn't feel right." Paying attention to such feelings can eliminate 95 percent of life's sloppy decision trees, allowing us to focus on a narrower range of choices, which then can be made intellectually. Without the ability to attend to how things feel, we are rudderless in life.

Self-awareness gives you the capacity to reconcile decisions with your deepest values, your sense of purpose, your mission. What matters to you? Is this decision in keeping with that? In addition to better decision making, self-awareness is essential to realistic self-assessment. While the arrogant, tuned-out leader protects him- or herself with blind spots, effective leaders know their strengths, their limits, and their weaknesses. Another leadership ability based on self-awareness is self-confidence. If you are sure in your heart that you're pursuing the right course of action, based on what your inner voice tells you, then you'll have self-confidence. You will be able to lead assertively, with strength. That's the source of courage in leadership.

2. *Managing emotions.* All effective leaders learn to handle the internal world of feeling, particularly the big three: anger, anxiety, sadness. Managing one's emotions is a matter of controlling one's impulses—and that turns out to be a decisive life skill.

In one famous study at Stanford University, four-year-olds who showed self-control (measured by their ability to wait several minutes to get two marshmallows rather than grabbing one immediately) showed remarkable differences from children with less control. Fourteen years later, as these same kids were graduating from high school, researchers found that those who waited were more emotionally stable, coped better with stress, were better liked, better motivated, and more goal-oriented than their counterparts. But the most stunning finding was completely unexpected: The children who waited compared to those who grabbed had an astonishing 210-point advantage on their college admissions tests, the SAT, out of a possible 1600. According to the Educational Testing Service, 210 points is larger than the difference between children from the poorest and the wealthiest families or between the children of parents with no high school education and those whose parents have advanced degrees.

Why should impulsivity so dramatically diminish a child's ability to learn? In school—or in the workplace—emotional agitation intrudes on working memory, the brain's ability to focus and pay attention. In short, stress makes people stupid because it leaves them with less attention to bring to the moment. That is why a leader's ability to manage emotions is crucial. One study of a large retail chain, for example, showed that store managers who could best handle stress and manage emotions had the highest profitability per square foot of stores.

When the Center for Creative Leadership updated its study of leaders who lost their jobs or started to stagnate, they found two main reasons: the failure to adapt to change and the failure to lead a team. Both relate to emotional intelligence and the ability to manage stress. Impulsivity is especially dangerous for leaders, whose abuse of their power over others can take the form of sexual harassment, financial wrongdoing, or simply brutish behavior. Self-control, clearly lacking in such cases, is the basis for integrity, conscientiousness, and trustworthiness. These are essential for every successful leader.

3. *Motivating others.* The root meaning of *motive* is the same as the root of emotion: *to move.* And what moves us to action is emotion. The goals that guide us, that shape our perception and memory, are rooted in strong feelings. One of the most important motivational abilities is optimism, which allows us to take setbacks in stride. There is a big difference in the emotional makeup of optimists versus pessimists. Pessimists see a setback as signifying some flaw in themselves that can't be overcome; they therefore tend to give up. Optimists see a setback as due to something they have the power to change; they try again. In a study at Metropolitan Life, the company agreed to hire a group of salespeople who scored high in a test of optimism but didn't fit the normal skills profile. In a thankless job requiring the ability to handle rejection—making cold calls by phone—the optimists showed far more perseverance and outperformed other new hires.

If you're leading an organization or team that suffers a set-back, everyone watches to see how you react. You've got to be the optimist if you're going to accept a setback, learn from it, carry on—and inspire others to do the same.

4. *Showing empathy.* The flip side of self-awareness is the ability to read emotions in others. After all, people seldom tell us in words what they're feeling; they tell us in tone of voice, in pacing, in gestures and facial expressions. Some people are better at reading these cues than others, but an inability to identify and empathize with others is a problem for anyone who wants to be a good partner, parent, colleague, or leader.

To take an extreme case, criminal sociopaths lack empathy. But so do organizational sociopaths. In almost any organization there are people who are purely self-interested, who don't care about anything other than their own success. If such people move into leadership positions, the organization is in real trouble, because the leaders are supposed to safeguard the organization's mission and serve the common good.

Lack of empathy is also destructive to group performance. If you're the recipient of contempt or disrespect, you suffer a huge amygdala hijack, according to research by psychologist John Gottman. Heart rates can go up 30 or 40 beats per minute; people say it's overwhelming, and they will do anything they can to end it. Often that means they tune out. People whose bosses blow up at them almost always say, "After that I didn't care what happened to the company" or "After that I'd quietly sabotage things." No leader can afford that. The signs of damage won't be immediately visible; they're silent, insidious, and create a ripple of dysfunction around that leader.

When we empathize, on the other hand, we provide a clear channel, putting aside our own agenda, so we can resonate with the other person; we're tuning into them by tuning into ourselves. If we are out of touch with how people are feeling, then our judgment is off. One of the most brilliant moves a leader can make—and what establishes people as natural leaders in a group—is to sense the unstated feelings of everyone in the group and to articulate them for the first time.

Empathy is also the basis for leveraging workforce diversity. Leaders who get to know people from other groups as people better manage diversity, because familiarity brings empathy. Likewise, empathy is essential to the effective coaching and development of others, another key leadership skill.

5. *Staying connected.* Emotions are contagious. There is a secret economy that passes among us all, a tacit part of every interaction, that makes each of us feel a little better or a little worse. If you're a leader, you have more emotional power than most people because people pay closer attention to you. Your emotions will ripple through a group, which is a great leverage point—if you can manage your emotional state. If you're enthusiastic, energetic, optimistic, then people in the group will respond in kind. If you're angry, arrogant, or rude, it's toxic for the group. Emotions are not only contagious, they spread from the top down.

Thinking positively, resolving conflicts, understanding relationships—in short, skillfully connecting with others—is especially powerful in maximizing the potential of teams. There are three levels of team performance. A poorly performing team does no better than the individual average. A well-performing team outperforms the individual average. But a superlative team produces results that are better than what even the most gifted member of the group is capable of. That's a group in synergy; it has what Warren Bennis calls organized genius. And the strongest predictor of such performance is the harmony of the group, the trust of the group, the sense of team identification. It is the group's emotional intelligence.

Raising Your EQ

Every leader must understand the need to select for, promote for, reward, and enhance people's emotional intelligence. The good news is, unlike IQ, EQ can be learned (see "Teaching Emotional Intelligence"). Emotional intelligence rises as we grow older. There's an original window of opportunity in childhood to develop EQ, because the emotional regulatory centers are the last part of the brain to mature. Not until age 15 or 16 do the prefrontal circuits that orchestrate emotional response become fully developed. If you can help children get it right early in life, they'll have it right for life.

What about adults? The brain remains plastic throughout life and shapes itself through repeated experience; if you have an ability that needs strengthening or you work with someone who

Teaching Emotional Intelligence

Changing an emotionally deficient individual or organization takes bold leadership. Deep behavioral change, which affects top leaders as well as the rank and file, is possible only if there is a critical mass of support within the company. If it doesn't exist you have to do what any change leader does—make your case, build alliances, and create a climate and an infrastructure that supports change.

(continued on the next page)

Identifying Those in Need

There are tests available that purport to measure emotional intelligence. But most self-tests are flawed. First, if people lack self-awareness, what do you make of their answers to the test? Second, if you look, for example, at empathy, the research shows that if you ask people how empathic they are and then compare the answers to more objective measures of empathy, you find zero correlation. But if you ask friends and associates how empathic someone is, you get a very high correlation. Thus, 360-degree assessments of emotional competence can be powerful development tools. Many such measures are emerging and will improve in the future. (I've just designed one that assesses emotional intelligence in leaders.) Leaders are well served by becoming more aware of themselves and of their impact on others.

Coaching for Results

If someone is repeatedly overreacting or negatively affecting their work or that of others, you can do several things. First, address the problem in private, at a time when you can both communicate thoughtfully. Speak with sensitivity, trying not to put the person on the defensive. And present some convincing evidence of the problem, such as feedback from other people—specific incidents and their consequences. Present a positive, hopeful scenario in which one's actions can change for the better. Finally, give the person a program for doing that. Don't just say "you can do better," but "and here's what you can do."

needs to improve some emotional competencies, it can be done—but it takes a new model of learning. We don't learn to change behavior by attending a classroom lecture. It takes sustained effort, organizational support, and an understanding of how the emotional brain functions.

Every emotional reaction pattern is supported by an underlying set of brain circuitry. If it's a negative pattern—if people lack initiative, lose their temper, behave arrogantly—you can do two things to help those people change. You first have to break the original, automatic behavior, which was probably learned in childhood. You then have to replace it with a positive response—to assert one's views in a meeting or to count to 10 in a moment of anger. That process takes a lot of work, commitment, and motivation on the part of both the teacher and the learner. You cannot bring in a trainer for a one-day seminar on how to improve your listening skills, for example. Rather, you need to give people a specific goal and a structure for learning. They must know what they're trying to accomplish, and they must practice it not just in their work but in all of their life. You need a learning plan for people, which they themselves help construct. And you need to support them with coaching, clear expectations, and positive work assignments.

The opportunities for emotionally intelligent leaders to make an impact are enormous. The bad news is, emotional intelligence is on the decline. A study of 3,000 American children found that for 15 years, between the mid-1970s and the late 1980s, children declined in emotional intelligence abilities across the board. They were more impulsive, more disobedient, more angry, more lonely, more sad. They declined in 42 measures, as reported by parents and teachers, and improved in none. It's a strong and a troubling trend, exacerbated by social and technological forces. Parents have less time to spend with their children, and today's video-digital generation is spending less time than any other interacting with others—which is the only way one develops emotional intelligence. The cohort that declined so precipitously in emotional intelligence, now in their 20s, is today's entry-level workforce. Leading with, and thereby teaching, emotional competency is essential to all organizations, and to society.

Max Weber, the great German sociologist, observed that before the rise of the modern organization, emotions were part of work. People worked at home, or in others' homes, and their working lives were based on human interactions. With the rise of modern organizations, emotions became taboo in the workplace. But you can't leave your emotions at home; they enter the workplace one way or another. That emotional undercurrent, ignored at great expense by managers, is being rediscovered. The next wave of emotionally intelligent organizations—flattened, open, and interconnected as they are—will be more deliberate about including our emotional lives in a positive way. Leaders will always have to deal with destructive or self-defeating emotions, but that is better than driving emotions underground, where they sabotage organizations from within.

Leaders can accomplish little without understanding and engaging the qualities of the heart. The changes that organizations are now demanding of their people call for even higher levels of commitment, compassion, caring, and vitality. If we forget the impact our actions have, especially during times of transition, we will cripple our workplace. But when we bring to work our own best selves, and appeal to the best in others, we as leaders can create not just more humane but more effective institutions.

Daniel Goleman is CEO of Emotional Intelligence Services in Sudbury, Massachusetts. A psychologist who has reported on behavioral and brain sciences for the *New York Times* for 12 years, he is author of the best-selling *Emotional Intelligence*. His latest book is *Working with Emotional Intelligence*.

5

The Trouble with Humility

Patrick Lencioni

A leader who is self-effacing and lacks charisma may fail to inspire confidence. A charismatic leader who believes that he or she is more important than others eventually will lose followers. To inspire both loyalty and excitement, a leader needs to couple humility with charisma. Both can be developed through reflection, feedback, and an emphasis on authenticity.

I once worked with a CEO who was a humble leader. I'll call him Alan.

I say Alan was humble because in his heart he believed that he was no better than the employees in his company. Whether it was the receptionist, a janitor, or one of his direct reports, Alan spoke to everyone the same way. No condescension, no paternalism, no arrogance. Every employee received the same tone, the same attention, the same courtesy from Alan, and people respected and admired him in return.

But don't get me wrong. Alan wasn't dynamic. In fact, he was somewhat plain; his critics would even say bland.

Whenever he gave a speech, employees would lean over to me and say, "When are we going to get Alan some coaching for his public speaking?" We all labored with him as he paused, stammered, looked down at his notes.

When Alan entered a room, people didn't really notice him, and that was his preference. The way he carried himself, his general demeanor, gave no indication that he was a person of importance, not to mention the CEO.

One day Alan stopped by the marketing department to speak to one of his vice presidents. He arrived at the VP's office at the same time as one of the company's new employees, who reached out her hand and said, "Hi, I'm Mary. I'm the new advertising co-ordinator." Alan smiled. "Nice to meet you, Mary. I'm Alan." Mary asked, "And what do you do, Alan?" With a tone that sounded more like a marketing intern than a chief executive, Alan simply replied, "Oh, I'm the CEO."

In spite of his low-key attitude and lack of charisma, Alan built a company from scratch that reached almost a billion dollars in revenue. He received numerous awards for entrepreneurship and accomplishment in business. What's more, Alan's company was known for having higher employee and customer loyalty than any other in the industry.

How did Alan accomplish all of this without a forceful personality? Certainly, part of Alan's success can be attributed to his intelligence. He had a way of sitting quietly during his staff meetings and saying almost nothing. While everyone else was advocating their points and positioning themselves to say something smart, Alan usually appeared to be tuned out of the conversation. When everyone had finally exhausted their opinions, Alan would succinctly summarize their reasoning and recommend a course of action that his reports immediately recognized as the best possible solution. His lucidity was made all the more impressive by the subdued nature of his personality.

In addition to his deceptive intellect, Alan had an unquestionably strong work ethic. He maintained a steady, persistent drive for results regardless of the challenges that confronted him. While Alan's intelligence and hard work certainly contributed to his success, they did not differentiate him from others. Most CEOs I've known are smart and work long hours, but that doesn't make them successful. What set Alan apart was his unmistakable humility, something that came to be valued by customers, partners, vendors, and employees alike. Anyone who knew Alan developed an affection for him and his company that easily transcended any shortcomings in his style. There is no question that Alan's authenticity provided the fuel for his organization's growth.

But there was a limit to Alan's success. As his company grew, his drawbacks became more costly to the business. Most new employees didn't get the opportunity to know Alan personally, so they never developed the loyalty to him that others did. And when they heard Alan speak to large groups, their sense of disappointment could not be offset by his hidden humility. "*This* is the Alan we've been hearing about?" Confidence in his ability to lead the organization began to wane.

As Alan's company grew and took on a higher profile in the market, his competitors began taking shots at him. Essentially, they were calling him out for a fight, but Alan had little interest in such public displays of competitiveness. In fact, he didn't like dealing with the press, and when he did make television appearances, his performance was less than impressive.

When I tried to help Alan find opportunities to make symbolic gestures to build his esteem in the eyes of employees, he seemed puzzled. What I came to realize later was that deep down inside, Alan simply could not fathom why employees cared so much about his actions. After all, in his mind he was no better than they were.

On the day that the board of directors bumped Alan upstairs to the chairman's office, he came by my office to break the news to me. I could not help but feel that deep amid his disappointment and sadness was a sense of relief. "I'm not the kind of person who likes to debate people on TV," he told me. "If that's what it takes, then maybe I'm not what they need."

Although employees know he lacks charisma, Alan is still revered by them for his character, his authenticity, his accomplishments, and his modesty.

But that's the trouble with humility; sometimes it makes it hard for a person to be a charismatic leader.

The Charismatic Leader

I once knew a chief executive of a very large organization who *was* a charismatic leader. We'll call her Zoe.

I say she was charismatic because she realized that her *actions* were more important than those of the people she led. As a result, Zoe was always aware of herself, and acted in a way that inspired people. Whether she was giving a speech, sitting in on a meeting, or walking the halls among employees, Zoe made the most of every encounter.

She knew how to show empathy, disappointment, excitement, and anger in a way that often moved people. She was self-deprecating much of the time, but celebrated the achievements of her organization with exuberance and flair. As a result, most employees loved to listen to Zoe's speeches and to be in meetings with her. In their minds, Zoe was a classic leader, and a good one.

Zoe's accomplishments were considerable. She achieved for her organization a higher profile in the industry than it would have merited based on performance alone. Through her magnetism and charm, she was able to fend off skeptical analysts and critics and establish herself as a masterful spokesperson in the industry. Her personal profile soared.

But there were exceptions to Zoe's ability to charm people, and they were important ones. The people who knew her best, her direct reports and others close to her, could not be mesmerized by Zoe the way most employees and outsiders were. Although they certainly appreciated her ebullient personality, they were often subtly disappointed by her actions, especially when she wasn't "on." These miscues were particularly disconcerting in contrast to her public persona.

It was clear to those who knew her best that Zoe regarded herself as inherently more important than the people she was chartered to lead. She arrived late to meetings purposefully, to make an entrance and avoid having to wait for anyone else. She used company resources to purchase expensive items for her office at a time when she was cutting costs in other parts of the organization. She made comments about employees that flew in the face of her public statements about respect for coworkers. And she was prone to fits of anger behind closed doors.

With the aid of a potent truth serum, I'm sure Zoe would have defended herself by saying, "Of course I'm more important than the people I lead. I'm smarter than most of them, I've taken more risks in my career, and no one else can do my job." All of which would have been true, to a certain extent.

Gradually, Zoe's ability to lead diminished among her direct reports. Her influence was strongest among the masses, those employees with limited personal exposure to her. As a result, she looked for more and more opportunities to address those people. She knew that her charisma could win them over.

She was right, until results began to slip. Almost immediately, it became harder and harder for Zoe to maintain her public persona. She found that her standing among the masses, although it had been extremely high, was paper-thin. As the organization struggled, general opinion of Zoe collapsed remarkably quickly, leaving her with a legacy of "all talk, no action."

When asked to assess Zoe's qualities as a leader, those who knew her came to the conclusion that she lacked something essential in a good leader. As skilled as she was at the art of feigned self-deprecation, Zoe did not have a humble bone in her body. "And why should I be humble?" I'm sure she would have said under the influence of that truth serum. "People are watching every move I make—I must be important."

But that's the trouble with charisma—it can make it difficult to be humble.

The Tyranny of the Or

In *Built to Last*, James Collins and Jerry Porras describe a phenomenon they call the "tyranny of the or." Essentially, it is the inability to hold two seemingly opposing ideas in mind simultaneously. For example, companies often mistakenly believe they must choose between opposing forces like long-term profit and short-term revenue growth, or concern for employees and concern for shareholders. Great companies, according to Collins and Porras, are able to adhere to both sides of a given issue, and therefore avoid the "tyranny of the or."

Alan and Zoe personify the opposite ends of the leadership see-saw where humility and charisma sit, creating a potential for the "tyranny of the or." Remember, I have defined humility as the realization that a leader is inherently no better than the people he or she leads, and charisma as the realization that a leader's actions are more important than those of the people he or she leads.

As leaders, we must strive to embrace humility and charisma. The problem is that, like a see-saw, when we try to raise our ability in one behavior, the other tends to drop.

Imagine Alan focusing on his "charismatic skills" as a leader. Better speeches. A comfortable television persona. The kind of behavior that turns heads in a room.

Assuming that he could pull this off, Alan would almost certainly begin to see himself in a different light. He would receive more attention than he did before. Being human, that would tempt him to think of himself more favorably. And there is a good chance that his humility would suffer.

If this sounds simplistic, we should consider the moments in our careers when we've been at our peak as a "public, charismatic leader." During these times it is sometimes difficult to maintain our sense of humility. All of us are susceptible to believing the praise and accolades that we receive, even when that praise comes from people who have a vested interest in winning our approval—unless we're lucky enough to go home to a spouse or children who can bring us back to earth.

Sam Nunn, the former U.S. Senator from Georgia, recounted how his wife restored his humility when he returned from a 1994 diplomatic mission to Haiti where he helped avert a bloody conflict. You can just imagine how he must have felt after accomplishing something of that magnitude that benefited so many people. A temporary loss of humility certainly would have been understandable.

But when he crawled into bed with his sleeping wife after a middle-of-the-night return flight from the Caribbean, she rolled over and in a barely coherent voice said, "Sam, will you clean the pool tomorrow? It's full of leaves." Humility restored.

Unfortunately, some of us are never asked to clean pools. One day we wake up and (perhaps) realize that we've lost the fundamental sense of humility we once had.

On the other end of the see-saw, imagine Zoe, through a personal setback or brutally honest feedback, coming to see that she is no better than the guy who empties her trash at night. If she were truly able to internalize this concept, chances are she would develop a reluctance to be the demonstrative leader that she was before. Certainly, her ego-driven motivation would be reduced, which would have a significant impact on her behavior.

The False Promise of Balance

Balance is not the answer. Part of the problem with the tyranny of the or is that we sometimes try to balance the opposing forces by compromising both in some way. This is the stuff of mediocrity.

If Alan were to trade even a little of his humility for some measure of charisma, he would risk destroying the humble core of his credibility as a leader. Unfortunately, rebuilding that core is a lot harder and takes more time than tearing it down.

Similarly, if Zoe were to trade some of her charisma for a little humility, she might well risk her ability to lead. And her credibility would deteriorate more quickly than Alan's. A humble leader is given the benefit of the doubt far more often than a charismatic leader, whom constituents like to see humbled from time to time. The daunting challenge confronting Alan and Zoe, and all leaders to some extent, is a simple but difficult one. A humble leader must find a way to become more charismatic without sacrificing humility. A charismatic leader must find a way to develop a sense of humility without sacrificing the ability to move others.

Theoretically, there is nothing preventing them from avoiding the tyranny of the or and developing greater humility and charisma simultaneously. However, it is extremely difficult to do in reality.

What's a Leader to Do?

The first step in taking on this challenge is to assess where on the leadership see-saw we fit (see "What Kind of Leader Are You?"). Even if we are able to confidently assess ourselves, it is important to get feedback from others. This not only provides evidence for our self-assessment, but can reinforce behavioral change.

Charismatic leaders who survey their constituents or, better yet, sit with them and discuss the ups and downs of their leadership style will likely be humbled by the experience. But because they are being open and public about their pursuit of humility, they will be more likely to maintain their charismatic edge. In fact, the process of being humbled publicly can actually increase a leader's ability to be charismatic, because it provides an impetus for authenticity.

Humble leaders who solicit feedback on their presentation skills or public persona will be seen as making a semi-public move toward greater charismatic leadership. While this will not

What Kind of Leader Are You?

This assessment requires you to honestly answer questions about your attitudes toward others. Certainly it will be easy to identify the "correct" answers. However, responding wishfully will not be helpful.

Remember, too, that the most effective leaders are not just humble nor just charismatic; they are both. Humility and charisma each offer important benefits to leaders and their organizations:

Benefits of Humility

Engenders trust and loyalty among direct reports and others who work closely with a leader

Allows more honest, unfiltered feedback from employees about what is happening in the organization

Minimizes politics and positioning within the organization

Benefits of Charisma

Inspires employees throughout the organization, even those who don't know a leader personally

Provides employees with a symbol to rally around during crises

Raises the profile of the organization

Answering yes to the following questions indicates your tendency to be either humble or charismatic. If you seem to do well in both categories, you may be an exceptional case—or you may be kidding yourself. Ask someone who can be completely honest with you to assess you along these same criteria.

Are you a humble leader?

Do you consider others in your organization to be as important as you are?

Do you respect their time as much as your own?

Do you hold yourself to the same standards that you set for others?

Are you genuinely interested in what lower-level employees have to say?

Do employees at lower levels of your organization approach you frequently and comfortably?

Are you sometimes reluctant to make grand public statements or take bold public action?

Are you often uncomfortable receiving praise?

Are you a charismatic leader?

Do you consider your actions to be more important than those of the people in your organization?

Do you look for opportunities to make public statements or take bold public action?

Are you aware of the extent that you actively manage your actions for public effect?

Do people tell you they enjoy hearing you speak?

Are people in your organization hesitant to give you frank and honest feedback? Are you sure?

Do you believe that your personal leadership is the key to your organization's success?

Are you comfortable receiving praise?

ensure that such skills develop, it will give the leader confidence and permission to step outside of his or her comfort zone and take bold action.

The single greatest impediment to raising both ends of the see-saw is the denial that both qualities are important. Humble leaders tend to discount the importance of charisma, labeling it phony or hokey. Charismatic leaders rarely discount the importance of humility publicly, but many of them privately believe that humility suggests weakness. A quote from Calvin Coolidge might help dispel that belief. "It is a great advantage to a president, and a major source of safety to the country, for him to know that he is not a great man."

Certainly, there are humble, quietly effective leaders who remain little known simply because of their humility. And there are more than a few chief executives who exude charisma (and arrogance) and who achieve much. But the exceptional leaders—we know them when we see them—combine the best of both worlds. They share an ability to inspire loyalty *and* excitement. Whatever a leader's tendency, success requires that he or she find a way to genuinely appreciate the need for both sides of the leadership see-saw—and find a way to break it in the middle and raise both ends at once.

Patrick Lencioni is president of The Table Group, an organizational development and executive coaching firm. Previously, he was a senior executive at Sybase Inc., Oracle Corporation, and Bain & Company. He is also a screenwriter and the author of *The Five Temptations of a CEO* and *Obsessions of an Extraordinary Executive*.

6

Mission as an Organizing Principle

C. William Pollard

Leaders must communicate their organization's mission to all parts of the organization. The mission provides a reference point, an anchor, and a source of hope in times of change. When it connects with people's values, it brings purpose and meaning to those who are fulfilling the mission and provides the impetus for creativity, productivity, and quality in the work and in personal development.

To say that today's leaders must learn to initiate rapid and continuous change is to state the obvious. Such change is a fact of life. The problem is, the people who make up organizations are not built for rapid and continuous change. In the absence of a meaningful mission and purpose that transcends the change and includes a caring and nurturing of people, rapid change can bring discontinuity, dislocation, and demoralization.

People need a hope beyond the change. They need an anchor, a purpose that does not change and that provides meaning for their life and for their work.

What is the role of our organizations in responding to this need for meaning? What will be the social contract between an employer and employee as we move to the 21st century? Have

53

we defined the mission of our organizations to include bringing purpose and meaning to those who are fulfilling the mission? How do we measure the effectiveness of our organizations? Can our organizations become moral communities to help shape the human character and behavior of our people? Can our mission be an organizing principle?

The first job of leaders is to ask, and try to answer, such questions. But our ultimate job is to be champions of the mission of the firm and, more important, to live that mission. We also must recognize that our values and character will be tested in the process.

I ask these fundamental questions not as a philosopher or educator but simply as a businessperson—someone who, with my colleagues, is seeking to lead a fast-growing, dynamic service company.

ServiceMaster has experienced rapid growth, doubling in size every 3½ years for over 25 years, with systemwide revenues now exceeding $6 billion. Yes, we have experienced massive change. Over 75 percent of our current business lines we did not do just ten years ago. And we face the same pressures as every public company. Revenue and profits must be reported quarterly. The shareholders to whom we are responsible vote every day on our leadership—they have the choice to buy, hold, or sell.

But a business leader's success cannot be limited to the calculation of profit or a return on equity. My success must be measured by the 240,000 people with whom I work—the people who deliver value to customers and shareholders every day.

Much of our business may be seen as routine and mundane. We clean toilets and floors, maintain boilers and air-handling units, serve food, kill bugs, care for lawns and landscapes, clean carpets, provide maid service, and repair home appliances. Our task as leaders is to train and motivate people to serve so they will do a more effective job, be more productive in their work and, yes, even be better people.

But how does one go about motivating so many people—most of whom are scattered about the locations of our 10 million customers? Although we work hard at developing our training programs and management systems, no amount of training or management can effectively motivate others to serve. Unless we align the values of our people with the mission of the firm, and unless we continue to develop and care for people in the process, we will fail.

A Reason for Being

When you visit our headquarters in Downers Grove, Illinois, you walk into a large, two-story lobby; on your right is a curving marble wall, 90 feet long and 18 feet high. Carved in stone on that wall are four statements that constitute our mission: To Honor God In All We Do, To Help People Develop, To Pursue Excellence, and To Grow Profitably. It's a statement simple enough to be remembered, controversial enough to require continuous dialogue, and profound enough to be lasting.

The first two objectives are end goals. The second two are means goals. All of them provide a reference point for people seeking to do that which is right and avoid that which is wrong. Our goals remind us that every person has been created with dignity, worth, and great potential. They remind us, too, that our core principles, like the wall itself, do not change.

In a pluralistic society, some may question whether our first objective is an appropriate goal for a public company. However, we do not use that goal as a basis of exclusion. It is, in fact, the basis for our promotion of diversity, as we recognize that different people are all part of God's mix, in whatever way (and whether or not) they choose to worship.

Our beliefs do not mean that everything in the business will be done right. We experience our share of mistakes. But because of a stated standard and our reason for that standard, we cannot hide our mistakes. They are brought into the open for correction and, in some cases, for forgiveness.

The New World of Work

Fifty years ago pundits were predicting that by the year 2000 everyone would be enjoying a 30-hour work week. The balance of our time would be spent in rest and leisure. But now it seems that most of us work harder. Others retire earlier or are in transition because their job is no longer needed. We use words like downsizing and rightsizing to mask the reality that people lose jobs for reasons other than performance. In fact, it has been suggested that we now live in a post-job world.

In this new world of work we have found that people want to contribute to a cause, not just earn a living. When we create alignment between the mission of the firm and the cause of its people, we unleash a creative power that results in quality service to the customer and the growth and development of the people who do the serving. People find meaning in their work. The mission becomes an organizing principle of effectiveness.

While we work with many accomplished people seeking new ways to contribute, we also have many workers coming to us with little or no formal training, social skills, or understanding of standards of civility. As a result, the workplace is increasingly becoming—or must become—a place of training and education, a University of Work. The distinctions we once made between going to school during part of our life and then working for the other part are no longer meaningful. For all people, the lines between school and work are blurring.

As we recognize the importance of dealing with the whole person, we seek to link the performance of the task with the development of the person, and to assume responsibility for what happens to the person in the process. What are they becoming in their work? Are the task as defined, the tools as designed, and the training so provided contributing to or detracting from the work and the worker? Are there opportunities for personal and professional advancement? These questions force a self-energizing, self-correcting, ongoing process that is the basis for continuous improvement in how we serve customers.

Of course, any task can be seen as drudgery or self-expression. A given job, no matter how mundane, is not determinative. The difference is to be found within the person doing the task, in that part of our being that seeks a meaning for life and work. It is the desire to accomplish something significant. A person who sees a rewarding purpose and a genuine opportunity beyond the task can bring creativity, productivity, quality, and value to any job. The job of the leader, then, is to articulate a mission that brings deeper meaning to work, and to assure that the organization's mission is in alignment with people's own growth and development.

Bringing Meaning to Work

Why is Shirley Nelson, a housekeeper in a 250-bed community hospital, still excited about her work after 15 years? She certainly has seen some changes. She actually cleans more rooms today than she did five years ago. The chemicals, the mop, and the housekeeping cart have all been improved. Nevertheless, the bathrooms and the toilets are the same. The dirt has not changed, nor have the unexpected spills of the patients or the arrogance of some of the physicians. So what motivates Shirley?

Shirley sees her job as extending to the welfare of the patient and as an integral part of a team that helps sick people get well. She has a cause that involves the health and welfare of others. When Shirley first started, no doubt she was merely looking for just a job. But she brought to her work an unlocked potential and a desire to accomplish something significant. As I talked with Shirley about her job, she said, "If we don't clean with a quality effort, we can't keep the doctors and nurses in business. We can't serve the patients. This place would be closed if we didn't have housekeeping." Shirley was confirming the reality of our mission. She was in command of her work, of herself, and of her own small piece of our business. And in a very real sense she was leading me, by talking about her work, her customers, and her role in our shared mission.

Leading the Whole Person

People are not just economic animals or production units. Everyone has a fingerprint of personality and potential and desire to contribute. When we define people solely in economic terms, our motivational and incentive schemes tend to become mechanical and manipulative. We try to define a system that will idiot-proof the process, which can in turn make people feel like idiots. *Fortune* magazine recently described the soulless company as suffering from an enemy within, citing Henry Ford's quote as descriptive: "Why is it that I always get the whole person when what I really want is just a pair of hands?"

The scope of training must include more than teaching a person to use the right tools or to complete an assigned task within a defined period. It also must include how people feel about their work, about themselves, and how they relate to others at work or at home.

Thus, if I am involved in the leadership process, then as part of my training, I should also experience what it is like to do the hands-on work and to feel the emotions of those I am going to manage. That is why every manager in ServiceMaster spends time actually doing the tasks he or she will ultimately manage others to do.

Over 20 years ago, when I started as senior vice president responsible for the legal and financial affairs of the company, I spent the first three months of my training doing cleaning and maintenance tasks in hospitals, factories, and homes. It was a learning and serving experience that helped me to identify with the needs and concerns of our service workers. It was a great lesson in servant leadership and the role of a leader in implementing the mission of a firm. It has been a constant reminder that I must always be prepared to serve and should never ask anyone to do something that I am not willing to do myself. As a leader in such an environment, I should always be ready to be surprised by the potential of people.

A colleague tells of an experience that has been a great reminder to me of this point. It is often the custom for firms to hand out service pins in recognition of years of service. As my friend was involved in such an event, he was surprised by the response of one of the recipients. The young man opened the box, took out the sterling silver tie tack, said thanks, and with a wide grin proudly put the pin into his ear lobe, not on his lapel.

People are different, and we should never be too quick to judge potential by appearance or lifestyle. It is a leader's responsibility to set the tone, to learn to accept the differences of people, and to foster an environment where different people can contribute as part of the whole and achieve unity in diversity.

When Work Is Only a Job

Several years ago I was traveling in what was then the Soviet Union. I had been asked to give several talks on the service business and our company objectives. While I was in the city then called Leningrad, now St. Petersburg, I met Olga. She had the job of mopping the lobby floor in a large hotel that at that time was occupied mostly by people from the West. I took an interest in her and her task. I engaged her in conversation through an interpreter and noted the tools she had to do her work. Olga had been given a T-frame for a mop, a filthy rag, and a bucket of dirty water. She really wasn't cleaning the floor; she was just moving dirt from place to place. The reality of Olga's task was to do the least number of motions in the greatest amount of time until the day was over. Olga was not proud of what she was doing. She had no dignity in her work. She was a long way from owning the result.

I knew from our brief conversation that there was a great untapped potential in Olga. I am sure you could have eaten off the floor in her two-room apartment—but work was something different. No one had taken the time to teach or equip Olga. She was lost in a system that did not care. Work was just a job that had to be done. She was the object of work, not the subject.

But think back to Shirley—what makes her experience of work so different from Olga's? Yes, one was born in Chicago and the other in Moscow, and their cultures, languages, and nationalities were different. But their basic tasks were the same. They both had to work for a living. They both had limited financial resources. One was proud of what she was doing. Her work had affected her view of herself and others. The other was not, and had a limited view of her potential and worth.

The difference, I suggest, has something to do with how they were treated, loved, and cared for in the work environment. In one case, the mission of the firm involved the development of the person, recognizing their dignity and worth. In the other case, the objective was to provide activity and call it work.

Everywhere one looks today, there is more freedom and more choice in our lives—but also more confusion and uncertainty. A corporate mission cannot be viewed as a panacea, nor applied like a mathematical formula. It can, however, provide a foundation, a reference point for action. It offers a living set of principles that allows us to confront the difficulties and contradictions of work life. When our mission becomes an organizing principle, our organizations become communities of people caring for each other and for those they serve. As we continue to define and refine that mission and seek to lead in its fulfillment, let us not forget the people who are serving and making it happen—they are the soul of our organizations.

C. William Pollard is chairman of the ServiceMaster Company. ServiceMaster has been recognized by *Fortune*, the *Wall Street Journal*, and *The Financial Times* as one of the most respected companies in the world and is ranked the No. 1 service company among the Fortune 500. Pollard speaks, writes, and teaches on management and ethics, and is author of the bestselling *Soul of the Firm*.

7

The Art of
Chaordic Leadership

Dee Hock

*The first responsibility of a leader is to manage his or her
own character, integrity, humility, knowledge, words, and
acts. Refuting the idea that management is an exercise of
authority over those below, chaordic leadership is based on
followership—a voluntary response to a clear, constructive
purpose and compelling ethical principles. Chaordic leaders
focus upward and sideward as well as downward. They do
not dictate; they modify conditions that prevent synergy and
accomplishment.*

There was a time a few years back when for one brief moment the essence of leadership was crystal clear to me.
Strangely, it was after leaving Visa and moving to a small, isolated ranch for a life of study and contemplation, raising a few
cattle. I was attending to chores in the barn, comfortable and
secure from the wind howling about the eaves and the roar of
torrential rain on the tin roof. Through the din, I became aware
of the faint, persistent bellowing of one of the cows. Awareness
gradually rose that the bellowing was unusual.

Flashlight in hand, I plunged into the storm and worked my
way across the pasture in the direction of the sound. On the far

63

side, in the circle of light from the flash, I could make out Eunice, the huge, one-horned mother cow. Sheltered in the corral to await the imminent birth of her calf, she had somehow gotten out and sought a private place to give birth—unfortunately, on the brink of a steep bank fifteen feet above a flooded creek that raged through a ravine choked with poison oak and wild blackberry vines.

I raced to the spot and saw from trampled ground and smashed bushes what had happened. She had given birth. The calf, struggling to gain its feet, had slipped over the edge and plunged down the bank into the creek, then desperately tried to climb the sheer bank to get free of the water. Eunice had done all that she could, racing up and down the bank, bellowing and searching in vain for a way down. By the time I responded to her cries, the calf had been swept downstream beneath tangled vines and brambles.

Grabbing at limbs and bushes, I half fell, half stumbled down the sheer bank into the creek. Pushed by the rushing, icy water, I worked my way under and through the thickets and brambles. In a bend of the creek a hundred feet downstream, I spotted the exhausted calf fighting to keep its head above water. By the time I arrived, it had given up and was submerged.

I pulled it onto a shelf of rocks beneath the mass of tangled growth and began pumping its ribs trying to eject water and assist its breathing. It was a magnificent dark-red bull calf, the hair on its flank a mass of curls, its soft hoofs torn and bleeding from efforts to climb the bank. It revived a little and began to kick and struggle. Pocketing the flashlight I managed to heave it across my shoulders and began a struggle upstream toward the place where I had entered and might have a chance to climb out.

What does a one-horned mother cow have to do with leadership? The answer requires a bit of reflection. Let's begin with a few words about words. Words are only secondarily the means by which we communicate; they're primarily the means by which we think. One can scarcely think or talk of organizations or management these days without coming across what leading thinkers from many disciplines believe will be the principal science of the next century: the understanding of autocatalytic, nonlinear, complex adaptive systems, usually referred to as "complexity."

The word is much too vague to describe such systems. After searching various lexicons in vain for a more suitable word, it seemed simpler to construct one. Since such systems, perhaps even life itself, are believed to arise and thrive on the edge of chaos with just enough order to give them pattern, I borrowed the first syllable of each, combined them and chaord ("kayord") emerged.

By *chaord*, I mean any self-organizing, self-governing, adaptive, nonlinear, complex organism, organization, community, or system, whether physical, biological, or social, the behavior of which harmoniously blends characteristics of both chaos and order. Loosely translated to business, it can be thought of as an organization that harmoniously blends characteristics of competition and cooperation; or from the perspective of education, an organization that seamlessly blends theoretical and experiential learning. As I learned from the formation and operation of Visa, an early archetype of such organizations, they require a much different consciousness about the leader/follower dichotomy.

Leader presumes follower. Follower presumes choice. One who is coerced to the purposes, objectives, or preferences of another is not a follower in any true sense of the word but an object of manipulation. Nor is the relationship materially altered if both parties voluntarily accept the dominance of one by the other. A true leader cannot be bound to lead. A true follower cannot be bound to follow. The moment they are bound they are no longer leader or follower. If the behavior of either is compelled, whether by force, economic necessity, or contractual arrangement, the relationship is altered to one of superior/subordinate, manager/employee, master/servant, or owner/slave. All such relationships are materially different from leader/follower.

Induced behavior is the essence of leader/follower. Compelled behavior is the essence of all the other relational concepts. Where behavior is compelled, there you will find tyranny, however benign. Where behavior is induced, there you will find leadership, however powerful. Leadership does not necessarily imply constructive, ethical, open conduct. It is entirely possible to induce destructive, malign, devious behavior, and to do so by corrupt means. Therefore, a clear, constructive purpose and compelling ethical principles evoked from and shared by all participants should be the essence of every relationship in every institution.

A vital question is how to ensure that those who lead are constructive, ethical, open, and honest. The answer is to follow those who behave in that manner. It comes down to both individual and collective sense of where and how people choose to be led. In a very real sense, followers lead by choosing where to be led. Where an organizational community will be led is inseparable from the shared values and beliefs of its members.

True leaders are those who epitomize the general sense of the community—who symbolize, legitimize, and strengthen behavior in accordance with the sense of the community—who enable its shared purpose, values, and beliefs to emerge and be transmitted. A true leader's behavior is induced by the behavior of every individual choosing where to be led.

The important thing to remember is that true leadership and induced behavior have an inherent tendency to the good, while tyranny (dominator management) and compelled behavior have an inherent tendency to evil.

Over the years, I have had long discussions with thousands of people throughout many different organizations about management: aspirations to it, dissatisfaction with it, or confusion about it. To avoid ambiguity, I always ask each person to describe the single most important responsibility of any manager. The incredibly diverse responses always have one thing in common: they are downward-looking. Management inevitably is viewed as exercise of authority—with selecting employees, motivating them, training them, appraising them, organizing them, directing them, controlling them. That perception is mistaken.

The first and paramount responsibility of anyone who purports to manage is to manage self: one's own integrity, character, ethics, knowledge, wisdom, temperament, words, and acts. It is a complex, unending, incredibly difficult, oft-shunned task. We spend little time and rarely excel at self-management precisely because it is so much more difficult than prescribing and controlling the behavior of others. However, without management of self, no one is fit for authority no matter how much they acquire, for the more authority they acquire the more dangerous they become. It is management of self that should occupy 50 percent of our time and the best of our ability. And when we do that, the ethical, moral, and spiritual elements of management are inescapable.

Asked to identify the second responsibility of any manager, again people produce a bewildering variety of opinions, again downward-looking. Another mistake. The second responsibility is to manage those who have authority over us: bosses, supervisors, directors, regulators, ad infinitum. Without their consent and support, how can we follow conviction, exercise judgment, use creative ability, achieve constructive results, or create conditions by which others can do the same? Managing superiors is essential. Devoting 25 percent of our time and ability to that effort is not too much.

Asked for the third responsibility, people become uncertain. Yet their thoughts remain on subordinates. Mistaken again. The third responsibility is to manage one's peers—those over whom we have no authority and who have no authority over us—associates, competitors, suppliers, customers—one's entire environment, if you will. Without their respect and confidence little or nothing can be accomplished. Our environment and peers can make a small heaven or hell of our life. Is it not wise to devote at least 20 percent of our time, energy, and ingenuity to managing them?

Asked for the fourth responsibility, people have difficulty coming up with an answer, for they are now troubled by thinking downward. However, if one has attended to self, superiors, and peers there is nothing else left. Obviously, the fourth responsibility is to manage those over whom we have authority. The common response is that all one's time will be consumed managing self, superiors, and peers. There will be no time to manage subordinates. Exactly! One need only select decent people, introduce them to the concept, induce them to practice it, and enjoy the process. If those over whom we have authority properly manage themselves, manage us, manage their peers, and replicate the process with those they employ, what is there to do but see they are properly recognized and rewarded—and stay out of their way?

It is not making better people of others that leadership is about. In today's world effective leadership is *chaordic*. It's about making a better person of oneself. Income, power, and position have nothing to do with that. In fact, they often interfere with it.

The obvious question then always erupts. How do you manage superiors, bosses, regulators, associates, customers? The answer is equally obvious. You cannot. But can you understand them? Can you persuade them? Can you motivate them? Can you disturb them, influence them, forgive them? *Can you set them an example?* Eventually the proper word emerges. Can you *lead* them?

Of course you can, provided only that you have properly led yourself. There are no rules and regulations so rigorous, no organization so hierarchical, no bosses so abusive that they can prevent us from behaving this way. No individual and no organization, short of killing us, can prevent such use of our energy, ability, and ingenuity. They may make it more difficult, but they can't prevent it. The real power is ours, not theirs, provided only that we can work our way around the killing.

It is easy to test this chaordic concept of leadership. Reflect a moment on group endeavors of which you are an observer rather than participant. If your interest runs to ballet, you can undoubtedly recall when the corps seemed to rise above the individual ability of each dancer and achieve a magical, seemingly effortless performance. If your interest runs to sports, the same phenomenon is apparent: teams whose performance transcends the ability of individuals. The same can be observed in the symphony, the theater, in fact, every group endeavor, including business and government.

Every choreographer, conductor, and coach—or for that matter, corporation president—has tried to distill the essence of such performance. Countless others have tried to explain and produce a mechanistic, measurably controlled process that will cause the phenomenon. It has never been done and it never will be. It is easily observed, universally admired, and occasionally experienced. It happens, but cannot be deliberately done. It is rarely long sustained but can be repeated. *It arises from the relationships and interaction of those from whom it is composed.* Some organizations seem consistently able to do so, just as some leaders seem able to cause it to happen with consistency, even within different organizations.

To be precise, one cannot speak of leaders who *cause* organizations to achieve superlative performance, for no one can *cause* it to happen. Leaders can only recognize and modify conditions that prevent it; they perceive and articulate a sense of community, a vision of the future, a body of principle to which people can become passionately committed, then encourage and enable them to discover and bring forth the extraordinary capabilities that lie trapped in everyone struggling to get out.

Without question, the most abundant, least expensive, most underutilized, and most constantly abused resource in the world is human ingenuity. The source of that abuse is mechanistic, Industrial Age, dominator concepts of organization and the management practices they spawn.

In the deepest sense, distinction between leaders and followers is meaningless. In every moment of life, we are simultaneously leading and following. There is never a time when our knowledge, judgment, and wisdom are not more useful and applicable than that of another. There is never a time when the knowledge, judgment, and wisdom of another are not more useful and applicable than ours. At any time that "other" may be superior, subordinate, or peer.

Everyone was born a leader. Who can deny that from the moment of birth they were leading parents, siblings, and companions? Watch a baby cry and the parents jump. We were all born leaders; that is, until we were sent to school and taught to be managed and to manage.

People are not things to be manipulated, boxed and labeled, bought and sold. Above all else, they are not "human resources." We are entire human beings, containing the whole of the evolving universe, limitless until we are limited, whether by self or others. We must examine the concept of leading and following with new eyes. We must examine the concept of superior and subordinate with increasing skepticism. We must examine the concept of management and labor with new beliefs. And we must examine the nature of organizations that demand such distinctions with an entirely different consciousness.

It is true leadership—leadership by everyone—chaordic leadership in, up, around, and down that this world so badly needs, and Industrial Age, dominator management that it so sadly gets.

But what about Eunice, the one-horned cow? A frantic thirty minutes after shouldering the calf, I arrived, shaking, bruised, and bleeding from cuts and scratches, at the bottom of the cut bank where the calf had tumbled in. Legs braced against the force of the rushing water, I paused to recover breath and strength before trying to clamber out. Suddenly, over the sound of the pulse pounding in my ears, the rushing water, shrieking wind, and pelting rain, from directly overhead came a furious, heart-stopping roar. In stark terror, I let go the calf's front legs and fumbled for the flashlight. Another earth-shaking roar, then another. The light came on as I swung the beam in the direction of the sound.

Exhausted, thigh-deep in swirling, icy water with 60 pounds of kicking calf draped around its neck, 175 pounds of *Homo sapiens* stared in pure panic directly up into the blood-red eyes of three-quarters of a ton of frantic mother cow convinced I was butchering her baby and a ton of enraged bull determined to save his family. In that brief instant, as I stood eye to eye with nearly two tons of bovine fury, the essence of management was

On Chaordic Leadership

Many convictions about leadership have served me well over the years. Although each of these few examples could benefit from pages of explication, a few words may provide insight to chaordic leadership.

• *Power:* True power is never used. If you use power, you never really had it.

• *Human Relations:* First, last, and only principle—when dealing with subordinates, repeat silently to yourself, "You are as great to you as I am to me, therefore, we are equal." When dealing with superiors, repeat silently to yourself, "I am as great to me as you are to you, therefore we are equal."

• *Criticism:* Active critics are a great asset. Without the slightest expenditure of time or effort, we have our weakness and error made apparent and alternatives proposed. We need only listen carefully, dismiss that which arises from ignorance, ignore that which arises from envy or malice, and embrace that which has merit.

• *Compensation:* Money motivates neither the best people nor the best in people. It can rent the body and influence the mind but it cannot touch the heart or move the spirit; that is reserved for belief, principle, and ethics.

• *Ego, Envy, Avarice, and Ambition:* Four beasts that inevitably devour their keeper. Harbor them at your peril, for although you expect to ride on their back, you will end up in their belly.

• *Position:* Subordinates may owe a measure of obedience by virtue of your position, but they owe no respect save that which you earn by your daily conduct. Without their respect, your authority is destructive.

• *Mistakes:* Toothless little things, providing you can recognize them, admit them, correct them, learn from them, and rise above them. If not, they grow fangs and strike.

• *Accomplishment:* Never confuse activity with productivity. It is not what goes in your end of the pipe that matters but what comes out the other end. Everything but intense thought, judgment, and action is infected to some degree with meaningless activity. Think! Judge! Act! Free others to do the same!

• *Hiring:* Never hire or promote in your own image. It is foolish to replicate your strength. It is stupid to replicate your weakness. Employ, trust, and reward those whose perspective, ability, and judgment are radically different from your own and recognize that it requires uncommon humility, tolerance, and wisdom.

• *Creativity:* The problem is never how to get new, innovative thoughts into your mind, but how to get old ones out. Every mind is a building filled with archaic furniture. Clean out a corner of your mind and creativity will instantly fill it.

• *Listening:* While you can learn much by listening carefully to what people say, a great deal more is revealed by what they do not say. Listen as carefully to silence as to sound.

• *Judgment:* Judgment is a muscle of the mind developed by use. You lose nothing by trusting it. If you trust it and it is bad, you will know quickly and can improve it. If you trust it and it is consistently good, you will succeed, and the sooner the better. If it is consistently good and you don't trust it, you will become the saddest of all creatures; one who could have succeeded but followed the poor judgment of others to failure.

• *Leadership:* Lead yourself, lead your superiors, lead your peers—and free your people to do the same. All else is trivia.

simple and clear. First: manage myself and get mind, body, and emotions under control before they ceased to exist. Second: manage two tons of enraged bovine superiors who most certainly had power over me. Third: manage my environment and find a way out of the ravine. Fourth: and by far the least important, manage my only subordinate, the kicking calf. And, oh, how I wished the calf knew the theory and had managed himself, his superiors, and his environment—and not put the whole outfit into such an unholy mess in the first place.

What then happened in the middle of the night to Eunice, her calf, and a panic-stricken *Homo sapiens* in a ditch need not be told, for that is not the point of the story. But for those who must find a moral in every story it is simply this: *If you keep your wits about you, you can learn everything you need to know about leadership from a one-horned cow.*

Dee Hock is founder and coordinating director of the Chaordic Alliance, whose purpose is to develop, disseminate, and implement new concepts of organization. Hock is also founder and CEO emeritus of both Visa USA and Visa International, now a $1.25 trillion enterprise jointly owned by more than 20,000 financial institutions. He is a laureate in the Business Hall of Fame and author of *Birth of the Chaordic Age*.

8

Managing Quietly

Henry Mintzberg

Managing quietly involves knowing that a leader is not the sum total of an organization. It involves inspiring, encouraging, and enabling others by creating a culture of openness, trust, community, and energy. Quiet leaders are low-key but engaging and interactive. They tend to their organizations and spend more time preventing problems than fixing them. They infuse values and slow, profound change for which everyone takes responsibility while holding other things steady—a natural continuous improvement.

A prominent business magazine hires a journalist to write about the chief executive of a major corporation. The man has been at the helm for several years and is considered highly effective. The journalist submits an excellent piece, capturing the very spirit of the man's managerial style. The magazine rejects it—not exciting enough, no hype. Yet the company has just broken profit records for its industry.

Not far away, another major corporation is undergoing dramatic transformation. Change is everywhere, the place is teeming with consultants, people are being released in huge numbers. The chief executive has been all over the business press. Suddenly he is fired: the board considers the turnaround a failure.

Go back five, ten, twenty or more years and read the business press—about John Scully at Apple, James Robinson at American Express, Robert McNamara at the Defense Department. Heroes of American management all . . . for a time. Then consider this proposition: maybe really good management is boring. Maybe the press is the problem, alongside the so-called gurus, since they are the ones who personalize success and deify the leaders (before they defile them). After all, corporations are large and complicated; it takes a lot of effort to find out what has really been going on. It is much easier to assume that the great one did it all. Makes for better stories too.

If you want to test this proposition, try Switzerland. It is a well-run country. No turnarounds. Ask the next Swiss you meet the name of the head of state. Don't be surprised if he or she does not know: the seven people who run the country sit around a table, rotating that position on an annual basis.

Management by Barking Around

"Forget what you know about how business should work—most of it is wrong!" screams the cover of that book called *Reengineering the Corporation*. Just like that. "Business reengineering means putting aside much of the received wisdom of two hundred years of industrial management," say the authors. Never mind that Henry Ford and Frederick Taylor, to name just two, "reengineered" business nearly a century ago. The new brand of reengineering "is to the next revolution of business what the specialization of labor was to the last" (meaning the Industrial Revolution). Are we so numbed by the hype of management that we accept such overstatement as normal?

There is no shortage of noisy words in the field of management. A few favored standbys merit special comment.

• *Globalization:* The Red Cross Federation headquarters in Geneva, Switzerland, has managers from over fifty countries. The Secretary General is Canadian; the three Under Secretary Generals are British, Swedish, and Sudanese. (There used to be a Swiss manager, but he retired.) The closest I know to a global company is perhaps Royal Dutch Shell, most of whose senior management comes from two countries—twice as many as almost any other company I can think of. But still a long way from the Red Cross Federation. Global coverage does not mean a global mind-set.

And is "globalization" new? Certainly the word is. They used to call it other things. At the turn of the century, the Singer Sewing Machine Company covered the globe (and that included some of the remotest parts of Africa) as few so-called global companies do today.

• *Shareholder value:* Is "shareholder value" new as well, or just another old way to sell the future cheap? Is this just an easy way for chief executives without ideas to squeeze money out of rich corporations? This mercenary model of management (greed is good, only numbers count, people are human "resources" who must be paid less so that executives can be paid more, and so on and on) is so antisocial that it will doom us if we don't doom it first.

• *Empowerment:* Organizations that have real empowerment don't talk about it. Those that make a lot of noise about it generally lack it: they have been spending too much of their past disempowering everybody. Then, suddenly, empowerment appears as a gift from the gods.

In actual fact, real empowerment is a most natural state of affairs: people know what they have to do and simply get on with it, like the worker bees in a beehive. Maybe the really healthy organizations empower their leaders, who in turn listen to what is going on and so look good.

• *Change management:* This is the ultimate in managerial noise. Companies are being turned around left and right—all part of today's *managerial correctness*, which, in its mindlessness, puts political correctness to shame.

BusinessWeek, on October 28, 1991, wrote about the University of Michigan's four-week general management program, whose faculty "has consulted with such companies as AT&T, Eastman Kodak, and Philips," all in highly publicized turnarounds at the time. That experience, we are told, provides much of the course material. But then consider:

> *BusinessWeek* cover, February 2, 1998: "AT&T: New Boss. New Strategy. Will it work?"
>
> *Fortune* article, May 11, 1998: "Why Kodak Still Isn't Fixed"
>
> *Fortune* article, March 31, 1997: "Can He [the new CEO] Fix Philips?

Automobile companies sometimes have to recall their cars; do universities ever recall their students?

• *Leadership:* Notice the wording of two of these headlines: "Can *He* Fix Philips" and AT&T's "New Boss" (who, we are told, transformed a sluggish performer in his "first 100 days"). A subhead on the third article reads "Can CEO George Fisher's big new shake-up do the job?" The white knight will ride in on his white horse and fix it all. Except that these knights mostly ride into territory they have never seen. (That's why they hire consultants.)

On March 2, 1998, *Fortune* put on display "America's Most Admired Corporations." But the accompanying article said hardly anything about these corporations. It was all about their leaders. After all, if the corporations succeeded, it must have been the bosses.

Lest that not have been enough, another article touted America's most admired CEOs. One was Merck's Raymond Gilmartin: "When Merck's directors tapped Gilmartin, 56, as CEO four years ago, they gave him a crucial mission: Create a new generation of blockbuster drugs to replace important products whose patents were soon to expire. Gilmartin has delivered."

You would think he had his hands full managing the company. Yet there he apparently was, in the labs, developing those drugs. And in just four years at that. From scratch.

"There is, believe it or not, some academic literature that suggests that leadership doesn't matter," we are told by the astonished *Fortune* writer. Well, this academic is no less astonished: there are, believe it or not, some business magazines so mesmerized with leadership that nothing else matters. "In four years Gerstner has added more than $40 billion to IBM's share value," this magazine proclaimed on April 14, 1997. Every penny of it! Nothing from the hundreds of thousands of other IBM employees. No role for the complex web of skills and relationships these people form. No contribution from luck. No help from a growing economy. Just Gerstner.

How about this comment in the academic literature: A vision-driven philosophy can perpetuate "the myth that organizations have to rely on one or two unusually gifted individuals to decide what to do, while the rest enthusiastically follow." This approach encourages "cultures of dependence and conformity that actually obstruct the questioning and complex learning which encourages innovative action," reports organizational theorist Ralph Stacey. Tough to read? Tough. Think about it.

I chair a Masters of Practicing Management program for managers sponsored by their companies. The program sessions take place at different locations around the world, and our Japanese colleagues run the module called *Managing People, the collaborative mind-set.* "Shouldn't we be teaching some leadership?" I kept asking. They never disagreed; they just didn't teach leadership. Then one day, we had a discussion about different styles of managing. "We could teach that!" was the response. Then it hit me. Leadership, for the Japanese, is a *style* of managing; in America, it *is* managing. If we are going to get even remotely global, shouldn't we start by opening our minds to the narrowness of our own conception of management?

Years ago, Peter Drucker wrote that the administrator works within the constraints; the manager removes the constraints. Later, Abraham Zaleznik claimed that managers merely manage; real leaders lead. Now we seem to be moving beyond leaders who merely lead; today heroes save. Soon heroes will only save; then gods will redeem. We keep upping the ante as we drop ever deeper into the morass of our own parochialism.

Despite a jittery stock market, American business seems to be doing rather well right now. But unless it gets off its destructive kicks—the mindlessness of managerial groupthink, the mercenary "me" of shareholder value and executive compensation, all the noise and the hype—it will be in deep trouble. So much of this activity is deadening and just plain socially bankrupt. The common sense and cooperative enthusiasm of management practiced in some other parts of the world will eventually swamp it. Bear in mind that it is the Japanese economy and banking system that has been having trouble, not the Japanese style of managing corporations.

The Problem Is the Present

Let's go back to that book on reengineering, the same page quoted earlier: "What matters in reengineering is how we want to organize work *today*, given the demands of *today's* market and the power of *today's* technologies. How people and companies did things yesterday doesn't matter to the business reengineer" (italics added).

Today, today, always *today.* One hundred todays to turn around AT&T. Today's books that depend on and then ignore yesterday's pioneers. This is the voice of the obsessively analytic mind, shouting into today's wind.

But if you want the imagination to see the future, then you'd better have the wisdom to appreciate the past. An obsession with the present—with what's "hot" and what's "in"—may be dazzling, but all that does is blind everyone to the reality. Show me a chief executive who ignores yesterday, who favors the new outsider over the experienced insider, the quick fix over steady progress, and I'll show you a chief executive who is destroying an organization.

To "turn around" is to end up facing the same way. Maybe that is the problem: all this turning around. Might not the white knight of management be the black hole of organizations? What good is the great leader if everything collapses when he or she leaves? Perhaps good companies don't need to be turned around at all because they are not constantly being thrust into crises by leaders who have to make their marks today. Maybe these companies are simply managed quietly.

Managing Quietly

What has been the greatest advance ever in health care? Not the dramatic discoveries of penicillin or insulin, it has been argued, but simply cleaning up the water supply. Perhaps, then, it is time to clean up our organizations, as well as our thinking. In this spirit I offer a few thoughts about some of the quiet words of managing.

• *Inspiring*: Quiet managers don't empower their people—"empowerment" is taken for granted. They *inspire* them. They create the conditions that foster openness and release energy. The queen bee, for example, does not make decisions; she just emits a chemical substance that holds the whole social system together. In human hives, that is called *culture*.

Quiet managers strengthen the cultural bonds between people, not by treating them as detachable "human resources" (probably the most offensive term ever coined in management, at least until "human capital" came along), but as respected members of a cohesive social system. When people are trusted, they do not have to be empowered.

The queen bee does not take credit for the worker bees' doing their jobs effectively. She just does her job effectively, so that they can do theirs. There are no bonuses for the queen bee beyond what she needs.

Next time you hear a chief executive go on about teamwork, about how "we" did it by all pulling together, ask who among the "we" is getting what kind of bonus. When you hear that chief boasting about taking the long view, ask how those bonuses are calculated. If cooperation and foresight are so important, why have these few been cashing in on generous stock options? Do we take the money back when the price plummets? Isn't it time to recognize this kind of executive compensation for what it is: a form of corruption, not only of our institutions, but of our societies as democratic systems?

• *Caring:* Quiet managers care for their organizations; they do not try to slice away problems as surgeons do. They spend more time preventing problems than fixing them, because they know enough to know when and how to intervene. In a sense, this is more like homeopathic medicine: the prescription of small doses to stimulate the system to fix itself. Better still, it is like the best of nursing: gentle care that, in itself, becomes cure.

• *Infusing:* "If you want to know what problems we have encountered over the years," someone from a major airline once told me, "just look at our headquarters units. Every time we have a problem, we create a new unit to deal with it." That is management by intrusion. Stick in someone or something to fix it. Ignore everyone and everything else: that is the past. What can the newly arrived chief know about the past, anyway? Besides, the stock analysts and magazine reporters don't have the time to allow the new chief to find out.

Quiet managing is about *infusion*, change that seeps in slowly, steadily, profoundly. Rather than having change thrust upon them in dramatic, superficial episodes, everyone takes responsibility for making sure that serious changes take hold. (See "A Quiet Leader at Work.")

This does not mean changing everything all the time—which is just another way of saying anarchy. It means always changing some things while holding most others steady. Call this *natural*

A Quiet Leader at Work

How does one manage quietly? Henry Mintzberg spent a day shadowing John Cleghorn, CEO of the Royal Bank of Canada, the country's largest and most successful bank, with 53,000 employees and 1998 profits of $1.8 billion Canadian. (Note that Mintzberg is actually Cleghorn Professor of Management Studies at McGill University, a chair created to honor Cleghorn's efforts as head of a McGill fundraising campaign. This day of observation was agreed to before that appointment was made.) Excerpts of these observations suggest that effective leadership is low-key, engaging, and interactive.

John Cleghorn's style of management is unusual for someone in his position: he is very involved in operational details of the bank. He's been known to call from the airport to report that an automatic teller machine is not working. He sold the corporate jet—he says he was uncomfortable with it—as well as the chauffeured limousines. All senior executives, Cleghorn included, are expected to spend at least 25 percent of their time with customers and front-line employees. (As one measure of performance, Cleghorn carefully tracks how he spends his own time.) The bank's stock ownership plan has helped 89 percent of employees become shareholders. Senior executives must own one to two times their base salary in stock; Cleghorn himself must own three times.

During the day he spent time visiting front-line staff in two branch offices and met with institutional investors as well as regional managers. All those meetings were marked by his straightforward style and upbeat nature. This day was action-oriented—particularly in the level of detail he attended to, such as suggesting a change in the branch bank's signage.

In his meetings with employees, Cleghorn aimed to gather information, but also to send signals about the organization, whether by encouraging long-term employees, congratulating people for their presentations, infusing his energy into the organization, or constantly describing the values he finds important. Rarely did he exercise the CEO's prerogative of control on this particular day. Rather, his role was to encourage and enable, with regard to the individual (motivating and coaching), the unit (team building), and the organization at large (culture building).

His strategy process appeared to be one of *crafting:* to foster a flexible structure and open culture, to see the strategic implications of initiatives, and to integrate them with overall vision. That requires his detailed, nuanced knowledge of the organization.

Of course, this approach, based on rich, grounded information, does not make someone a strategist: that depends on one's capacity for creative synthesis. But I believe that such a style of managing is a prerequisite for developing strategic insights. It is the ability to move between the concrete and the conceptual—not only to understand the specifics but also to be able to generalize creatively about them—that makes a great strategist.

Such is the practice of management as a craft—low key, involved, warm, focused, perhaps quintessentially Canadian. It may not make the headlines, but it seems to work.

continuous improvement, if you like. The trick, of course, is to know what to change when. And to achieve that there is no substitute for a leadership with an intimate understanding of the organization working with a workforce that is respected and trusted. That way, when people leave, including the leaders, progress continues.

• *Initiating:* Moses supplies our image of the strategy process: walking down the mountain carrying the word from on high to the waiting faithful. Redemption from the heavens. Of course, there are too many people to read the tablets, so the leaders have to shout these "formulations" to all these "implementors." All so very neat.

Except that life in the valleys below is rich and complicated. And that is what strategy has to be about—not the neat abstractions of the executive suite, but the messy patterns of daily life. So long as loud management stays up there disconnected, it can shout down all the strategies it likes: they will never work. They just create that noisy "culture of dependence."

Quiet management is not about drinking champagne in Business Class (which has become more than just a place in an airplane); it is about rolling up sleeves and finding out what is going on. And it is not parachuted down on the organization; it rises up from the base. But it never leaves that base. It functions "on the floor," where the knowledge for strategy making lies. Such management blends into the daily life of the corporation, so that all sorts of people with their feet planted firmly on the ground can pursue exciting initiatives. Then managers who are in touch with them can champion these initiatives and so stimulate the process by which strategies evolve.

Put differently, the manager is not the organization any more than a coat of paint is what holds up a building. Louis Gerstner is not IBM and Percy Barnevik was not ABB (if he was, the company is in for trouble now that he's left). A healthy organization does not have to leap from one hero to another; it is a collective social system that naturally survives changes in leadership. If you want to judge the leader, look at the organization ten years later.

Beyond Quiet

Quiet management is about thoughtfulness rooted in experi-ence. Words like wisdom, trust, dedication, and judgment apply. Leadership works because it is legitimate, meaning that it is an integral part of the organization and so has the respect of every-one there. Tomorrow is appreciated because yesterday is hon-ored. That makes today a pleasure.

Indeed, the best managing of all may well be silent. That way people can say, "We did it ourselves." Because we did.

Henry Mintzberg is Cleghorn Professor of Management Stud-ies at McGill University in Montreal and professor of organiza-tion at INSEAD in France. Well known for his studies of strategic development and of managerial practice, Mintzberg is author or coauthor of ten books, including *The Rise and Fall of Strategic Plan-ning* and *Strategy Safari*.

9

Maintaining a Mission

Lessons from the Marketplace

David M. Lawrence

Facing the challenge of competing in the marketplace while remaining true to its social mission, Kaiser Permanente learned eight lessons for mission-driven organizations: (1) to employ sound business principles in order to do social good; (2) to reduce costs through continuous quality improvement; (3) to set strategic directions based on the mission; (4) to engage the workforce and be open to new ideas; (5) to align structure and governance for maximum agility; (6) to encourage innovation and flexibility; (7) to partner with stakeholders; and (8) to integrate services.

There is no denying the enormous impact of market forces on a mission-driven organization. In the health care industry, as in other industries, every organization must be competitive to survive. The turbulent marketplace is providing on-the-job training for people in all organizations. And we're discovering that lessons from the marketplace can be harnessed to enhance our social mission rather than diminish it.

Kaiser Permanente is what I know best. But the eight lessons that follow can apply to any mission-driven organization. First, a bit of background about Kaiser Permanente and the environment in which it operates.

Kaiser Permanente is the largest integrated health care organization, as well as the largest nonprofit organization, in the nation. We are a $15.5 billion enterprise with 90,000 employees, 28 hospitals, and more than 10,000 physicians serving 8.6 million members. Our roots go back to the 1930s, when the great industrialist Henry Kaiser started his own health plan for his companies' employees, from construction workers on the Grand Coulee Dam project to shipyard workers in California. It was a group practice with prepaid services and an emphasis on prevention—the forerunner of the modern-day health maintenance organization—and offered an innovative and affordable alternative to fee-for-service medical care. In 1945, we opened membership to the public and began operating as a nonprofit organization with a clear social mission: to improve the health of our members and our communities. Much of our initial early membership came from labor unions.

Our integrated health care financing and delivery system is made up of three entities: the nonprofit health plan, the nonprofit hospitals organization, and the 11 Permanente Medical Groups, locally based and organized as professional corporations or professional partnerships. These 10,000 physicians make all clinical decisions and set all clinical policies. The success of our enterprise is based on the strong partnership among the three entities.

In the 1990s, the economics of health care changed radically. First, big purchasers of health care services—private employers and government—waged a battle to combat annual double-digit increases in health care costs. Second, years of expansion by health care providers created excess capacity in health care services and facilities. This oversupply enabled the creation of managed care organizations—aggressive, well-financed companies that bought health care services at well below historic market prices, bundled and rearranged them in attractive packages, and then

resold them at a profit. Throughout the decade, mergers and acquisitions have continually changed the face of the industry. And
the rise of influential advocacy groups such as business consortia
and consumer organizations, combined with new legislative man-
dates, brought additional demands on providers and insurers.
Amid these changes, Kaiser Permanente has remained one of a
small handful of nonprofit HMOs; many nonprofit health care organizations in recent years have been purchased by or converted
to for-profit corporations. It has been, in short, a time of profound
change for the entire industry.

Events of the last decade provoked organizational "midlife
crises" for many mission-driven organizations, including Kaiser
Permanente. Was it possible to compete in the marketplace and
at the same time remain true to our social mission? We're by no
means finished answering this question, and we've gained some
wisdom—along with some bruises—along the way. Following
are eight lessons for mission-driven organizations to heed.

Lesson One: No Margin, No Mission; No Mission, No Margin

When I first became a senior executive at Kaiser Permanente,
people used to tell me varying accounts of the same story, in
which the leader of a nonprofit hospital would exhort the staff,
"No margin, no mission!" We may be social entrepreneurs—using
every dollar of net income to improve the health of our members
and our communities—but we need to employ sound business
principles to do social good. No matter how important the mission, it can't be achieved without sound financial management.

Our organization has had to learn this lesson the hard way.
We have endured two years of large financial losses—the first in
our history. We suffered the double whammy of keeping our rates

too low to support the actual costs of providing care, combined with unanticipated surges in membership that required care beyond our capacity to provide in-house. With our ongoing focus on continuous quality improvement and by making some major changes—selling unprofitable operations, developing innovative purchasing practices, and more accurate forecasting of industry and membership trends—we recorded a positive first quarter margin in 1999 and expect to end the year in the black.

The corollary to "no margin, no mission" is "no mission, no margin." Our mission—to improve the health of our members and our communities—remains our touchstone and represents an important source of confidence for our members. They know we're not in this to enrich shareholders or investors. To abandon our mission would be to abandon an important competitive edge.

Lesson Two: Continuous Quality Improvement Will Reduce Costs

Mission-driven organizations need only look at the success of corporations such as Motorola, Toyota, and 3M, known both for the quality of their products and their long-term results, to see that quality, cost, and waste are really a single issue. It is particularly apt for health care, where variation in practice and quality is high.

Don Berwick, MD, president of the Institute for Health Improvement, declares that "improvements in American health care are both feasible and can contribute to substantial double-digit reductions in the total costs of care." In the United States today, the sad fact is that your geography is your health care destiny. Medicare breast cancer patients in Elyria, Ohio, for example, receive breast-conserving surgery 48 percent of the time. Those in Rapid City, South Dakota, however, have the option of such surgery less than 2 percent of the time. The solution to high variation is to base decisions on the demonstrated effectiveness and benefit of specific treatments. (While most lay people assume this is how physicians practice already, the huge variation in practice shows this isn't always the case.)

Another disturbing example of the costs of poor quality is hospital medication errors. In his book *Demanding Medical Excellence*, Michael Millenson describes a 1991 study of the hospitals of New York State by researchers at the Harvard School of Public Health. They estimated that 180,000 people die each year as a result of in-hospital medication errors, of which 120,000 are preventable. This is the equivalent of a fully loaded jumbo jet crashing and killing 329 people every day of the year.

While quality improvement is needed throughout the health care industry, many efforts are beginning to make a difference. For example, our premature birth prevention programs have averted one in four premature deliveries. Babies get a healthier start by being carried to term, and neonatal intensive care—with costs more than ten times those of a full-term newborn nursery—has been reduced by 25 percent.

Continuous improvement efforts must also influence organizational practices. Using rigorous quality measurement tools, for example, our physicians set goals for annual improvements in immunizations, mammography, and other preventive care. In addition, we have begun linking compensation to group performance; simply put, doctors will be best rewarded when patients have the best outcomes.

Lesson Three: Set Strategic Directions Based on Your Mission

How does one's mission help set strategic decision making? For Kaiser Permanente, a 40-year history of sponsoring clinical research stems from our mission to improve the health of our members and the communities we serve. During the past two years alone, our researchers have authored or coauthored nearly 400 research publications and participated in more than 1,000 research studies. Each year, we commit 3 percent of revenue to improving the health of our communities. In recent years, our direct community benefit investments totaled between $300 million and $400 million, and have focused primarily on children, the uninsured, and health services research.

For an organization like New York's Common Ground Community, a clear and compelling purpose—to transform a squalid residential hotel in Times Square into safe low-cost housing—led the organization to address broader questions of homelessness and joblessness. Through strategic partnerships with area businesses, Common Ground operates the Times Square Jobs Training Program. Its training, counseling, and job placement services for hotel tenants are less expensive than most government-sponsored programs. And 78 percent of those placed—formerly chronically unemployed—remain employed after two years.

Lesson Four: Engage Your Workforce and Be Open to New Ideas

In the private sector, General Electric, one of the most competitive and admired corporations in the world, learned the value of employee engagement and capacity for change. A decade ago GE's stated mission—to be first or second in every market in which it competes—clearly depended on the ideas, energy, and commitment of the workforce. CEO Jack Welch's famous Work-Out program broke new ground in workplace dialogue and set new standards of accountability for both management and staff. In *The Human Equation*, Stanford Business School professor Jeffrey Pfeffer presents compelling research showing that more open, participative management practices produce better results than purely financially driven approaches.

In a service industry like health care, employee participation is essential to quality improvement and organizational performance. Yet as a marketplace grows increasingly competitive, labor relations often grow more adversarial. That was our experience. As one of the most highly unionized organizations in the nation, with some 50 collective bargaining agreements covering 70 percent of our workforce, we have had our share of labor-management turbulence.

However, employees demand and deserve a voice in the future of an organization. In 1997, the AFL-CIO and Kaiser Permanente agreed to the most ambitious national labor-management partnership ever, covering 26 union locals across multiple markets. These unions represent 55,000 workers including nurses, optometrists, and pharmacists, as well as technical, clerical, and service workers. We have pledged to better the work environment and job security for workers, involving employees and their unions in decision making, and promoting KP as the health plan of choice for labor.

The partnership is one way we hope to gain new ideas. Another method has been infusing our organization with new blood at the senior management level. About one-third of Kaiser

Permanente's executives have been with the organization less than five years. This has been an intentional effort to balance the experience and perspectives of long-term Kaiser Permanente executives with people from outside our organization who bring fresh points of view. It is supported by two key mechanisms—an aggressive recruiting strategy and a redesigned professional development program for executive leadership. The goal is to invigorate our culture while keeping focused on our mission.

Lesson Five: Align Structure and Governance for Maximum Agility

A rapidly changing marketplace requires rapid response. An organization's board of directors can play an active role in shaping that response. Traditionally, our board was a caretaker for an organization that changed slowly. But, beginning in the early 1990s, we began shifting the board's focus to strategic issues, and we changed the composition of the board to bring in a broader range of perspectives and expertise. I now consider our board members to be my thought partners, and while, as an activist board, they demand more from me, they are helping me do a better job. For instance, the board has collaborated with management to integrate the formerly autonomous and disparate information technology operations across our organization nationally. It also has demanded that management develop more rigorous and focused capital investment decisions, as well as financial and performance control systems.

Our medical groups have also made governance changes. They formed the Permanente Federation, giving the various Permanente Medical Groups a more consistent voice, and helping our organization make faster decisions.

Lesson Six: Encourage Innovation and Flexibility

Although it can feel chaotic at times, and failures do occur, innovation must be encouraged if an organization is to remain competitive. In any large or complex organization, the challenge is to move best practices across local markets and throughout the enterprise.

Corporate skunk works, spin-offs, and job rotations are all strategies for promoting innovation. World-class companies like Nokia, which quickly gained dominance in the mobile phone market, achieve *strategic innovation* by asking managers throughout the organization to study, debate, and propose new ways to serve the market.

The ability to collect, manage, and make sense of available information is key. In the patient care arena, for example, our Care Management Institute studies clinical conditions such as asthma, diabetes, coronary artery disease, and depression, synthesizing knowledge from both within and outside Kaiser Permanente on the best clinical approaches. It then helps practicing physicians implement programs—tailored to the individual patient—by working with physicians and health care professionals at the local level.

An important technological innovation is the development of Kaiser Permanente Online, a restricted Web site that allows members to research health conditions and medications, get advice from a nurse or pharmacist, request appointments, join moderated discussion groups, and more. It started as a pilot project in 1997 with 1,000 Kaiser Permanente members in Silicon Valley, and is now available nationally to nearly all Kaiser Permanente members with Internet access.

Lesson Seven: Partner with Stakeholders

In recent years we have learned the value of forming partnerships with key stakeholders. By doing so, we are better able to meet purchaser and member needs. For example, we are now partnering with purchasers like CalPERS, the California state public employees' benefits system, and the Pacific Business Group on Health, a consortium representing key West Coast employers who purchase health benefits. We meet quarterly with CalPERS management to review our financial results and business plans. Similarly, we meet regularly with PBGH and are active participants in its ongoing quality measurement projects. It is one of many alliances we have with employers, community health organizations, and national consumer groups.

For small, community-based business and nonprofit organizations, partnership is even more essential. The Pain Management Program, sponsored by Children's Hope Foundation, helps children with HIV/AIDS cope with the often painful side effects of their medical treatment—pain that often was overlooked or undertreated by their caregivers. Working with 95 hospitals and community agencies, PMP has grown from a one-time symposium to a training program and seminar series that has benefited more than 2,000 children.

Project Health-line is a partnership between Phoenix House, a national substance abuse prevention program, and the Bridge, a New York City housing and rehabilitation service for the mentally ill. The program provides coordinated, on-site medical care to every Bridge resident. It has improved clients' physical and mental health, has reduced the costs of care to a hard-to-serve population, and led the Bridge to establish similar partnerships with other nonprofit agencies.

Lesson Eight: Integration Is Key

Integration of services gives providers the ability to manage variation and ensure greater continuity. This has been demonstrated again and again in manufacturing. GE has grown dramatically in recent years by providing training, maintenance, and technical support for the equipment it sells—everything from X-ray equipment to jet engines to entire power plants. Dell Computer revolutionized its industry by creating new, fluid relationships with both suppliers and customers, eliminating the need for dealers who often added little value. Amazon.com not only sells millions of books and CDs (and now almost any consumer product) but also has created a database that lets it track and cater to the tastes of individual customers.

But integration applies just as much to health care, where specialization can lead to fragmented (and, to the patient, bewildering) treatment. Kaiser Permanente's pediatric asthma management program is one response to this challenge. It is a jointly developed treatment plan that involves monitoring by the physician, instruction in use of home diagnostic tools, a 24-hour telephone advice line, and hospital emergency department staff trained to reinforce self-management, intervening with appropriate clinical support. This same integrated web of support works with chronic diseases, cardiac care, pregnancy care, or diabetes care.

On a larger scale, Kaiser Permanente's National Clinical Information System, currently under development, will allow all providers to determine at a glance when a diabetic patient is due for a foot or eye exam, or other checkup. It will show all the other health problems and medications associated with the patient. Best of all, diabetic patients will be involved in their own care through tailored health education and reminders of when it's time to see the doctor again.

The great irony about managed care is that most of it isn't. It manages contracts and benefit design, but not really health care delivery. True management of health care delivery requires system integration. That is still a rarity, in health care and in most other industries.

Strengthening Trust

Mission-driven organizations are in a unique competitive position. Yes, they must respond to market forces if they are to survive. Like any other business, they cannot be complacent. But they possess a treasure that must be carefully tended—the trust of their members and customers.

In these times of major change, organizations have choices, and those choices can serve to build—or erode—that trust. Do the choices we make as leaders involve employees in setting the direction of our organization? Do they resolve conflict with more collaboration and less acrimony to maintain the focus on organizational goals? Do they take chances with innovations that might fail? Do they partner with stakeholders to the mutual benefit of all parties? How we choose to meet today's challenges will determine the level of trust we attain, and therefore, our future success.

David M. Lawrence, MD, is chairman and CEO of Kaiser Permanente, the nation's largest nonprofit health care organization. He has also served as director of human services for Multnomah County, Oregon; on the faculty of the School of Public Health and Community Medicine, University of Washington; as an adviser to the Ministry of Health in Chile; and as a Peace Corps physician.

10

Closing the Strategic Generation Gap

A Conversation
with Christopher Bartlett

The old management model built around strategy, structure, and systems must be replaced by one based on purpose, process, and people. The scarce resource is now knowledge and expertise rather than capital. One of a leader's key tasks is to attract, motivate, and retain people who want to be doing something meaningful. Rather than being based on hierarchies of tasks and responsibilities, organizations should be built around three core processes: (1) bottom-up entrepreneurial initiative; (2) linking and leveraging assets in order to develop, diffuse, and apply initiatives and knowledge; and (3) continuous self-renewal. Bartlett states that the leader's role is changing from managing strategic content to creating an atmosphere that motivates and stretches achievement.

Few executives think about their job or carry it out as they did just a few years ago. Following are highlights of a conversation with Christopher Bartlett, a keen observer of the theory, practice, and history of management, about the changes he sees in the business environment and what they mean for the work of leaders.

Organizations in the 1990s have been strained by many forces. A truly global economy has demanded that companies capture large-scale efficiency and competitiveness, be responsive to national differences, and link their efforts around the world for rapid innovation. Meanwhile, the total quality management movement brought new standards that changed companies' operations and processes. The arrival of a service-based economy changed the ways companies deal with their consumers. The information age, privatization, deregulation, the convergence of industry boundaries, and the rise of a knowledge-based economy all created a widening gap between companies' strategic visions and their organizational and (more important) managerial capabilities.

There are lots of tools available to bring about the necessary changes, and unfortunately many organizations are using them all—downsizing, de-layering, restructuring, reengineering, organizational learning, empowerment, core competency analysis. All of these are powerful, but used as a random sequence of programmatic changes, they become little more than tune-ups for an organizational engine that needs replacement.

The problem is generational—and despite the hype about Gen-Xers versus Boomers, it has little to do with age. It has everything to do with deeply embedded management philosophy. Most of today's managers were raised on a 1920s model of management built around the powerful concepts of strategy, structure, and systems. We were taught that if we could find the right organizational form (for instance, the divisionalized structure pioneered by Alfred Sloan at GM) and install information, planning, and control systems that allowed us to manage that structure, then management could set strategy, allocate scarce capital resources, measure return, and prosper.

That model has served us well for 75 years but is now failing us. As a result, many leaders are trying to implement third-generation strategies through second-generation organizations with first-generation management practices.

Why Management Practice Lags Behind Strategy

One reason for this strategic generation gap is that, for most companies, capital is no longer the scarce resource. Global financial markets now provide more capital than companies can absorb. There's more money being taken out of the stock market through stock buy-backs than is being issued in new public offerings. Companies awash in capital are generating the current wave of mergers and acquisitions, and their motivation is not always obvious. Often they are trying to buy not only market share and gross revenue but also new ideas and initiatives, which are increasingly difficult to generate internally.

Today's scarce resources are the information, knowledge, and expertise necessary to compete in an information age and a service-based economy. Those resources reside deep in the organization, in the minds of individuals and in the relationships among them as they sense and respond to a fast-changing external environment. Yes, we still have to allocate capital, but that's no longer our main strategic constraint. The real challenge for management is how to develop and extend the knowledge necessary to create new initiatives, develop required capabilities, and renew the organization. The strategy, structure, and systems model is being overlaid by a new management philosophy based on purpose, process, and people as the core elements of successful enterprise.

The strategy-structure-systems model was designed to haul information to the top of the company, where the CEO could make strategic choices, allocate capital accordingly, and control against it. But as increasingly sophisticated information technology put a supercharger on management systems, executives were able to haul more and more complex information up through the organization. Yet those at the top could not possibly keep up with the rapid changes in their external environment, and companies found themselves drowning in data but starved for knowledge.

What It Means to Move
Beyond Strategy to Purpose

For decades, the strategy-structure-systems model provided a powerful way to frame the organization. Strategy became the means for allocating scarce capital resources across competing needs, based on analysis focused on product market positioning, profitability, growth, and shareholder returns. It was a rational, analytic process for making sound economic choices. But organizations are not just economic entities, they're also social institutions. For many people, much of the meaning in life comes from their engagement in their workplace. In the new economy, the senior leaders' most important task is to infuse the organization with a sense of purpose, personal engagement, genuine values, and collective identity.

We still need strategy, but if the scarce resource is knowledge and expertise, then the question is, how do we attract, excite, engage, motivate, and retain people who want not just to work for a company (with a sophisticated strategy) but to belong to an organization that's doing something important? People need to see the meaning in their work—that's why organizational visions and values have become so powerful. They allow organizations to think through not only "what do we want to aim for?" but "what do we stand for?"

Moving Beyond Structure to Process

In a world that's multidimensional and dynamic, it's foolish to create an organization that's one-dimensional and static. We need to build the organization not around a hierarchy of tasks and responsibilities but rather around a set of *processes* that define flexible roles and relationships. Yes, we may need to reengineer a business operation. But such efforts typically target specific functions—the order-entry process, for example—and too often lose sight of the bigger picture. Organizations that succeed in closing the gap between their managerial and strategic capabilities build their essential activities around three core processes:

• *Entrepreneurial initiative.* When those on the front lines are in closest contact with the fast-changing external environment and in control of the scarce knowledge and expertise, bottom-up initiative is a vital process that every organization must create. Those that have done so—companies like 3M, Canon, and ABB, for example—have developed powerful engines of sustainable competitive advantage.

Driving this process is the front-line manager. Historically, this individual was a loyal implementer who enforced orders and policies. Today, however, operating managers must be the champions of entrepreneurial initiative. Only they have the hands-on knowledge, expertise, and direct access to the new scarce resource in the organization—talent and ideas. That new role requires very different attitudes, knowledge, and skills—the ability to tolerate ambiguity, for example, as well as the capability, motivation, and tools to push entrepreneurial initiatives from the bottom up.

• *Linking and leveraging assets.* The old hierarchical structure with information, planning, and control systems was designed to allocate capital and measure financial performance. The vertical, financially driven information flows it created were well suited to an era when capital was the scarce resource; unfortunately the same patterns blocked the transfer of knowledge and expertise from one unit to another. The horizontally driven process of linking and leveraging key assets and resources is central to the task of developing, diffusing, and applying knowledge— the process at the heart of organizational learning. It implies the ability to take the expertise in one area, link it to an asset in a second area, locate information tracked by a third area, and deliver a product where the opportunity lies.

These challenges become the primary tasks of midlevel and senior managers—the people who can look across the organization and see where the assets, resources, and capabilities reside. They add value by developing the cross-organizational linkages that allow the company to recognize and leverage the new ideas and initiatives developed in entrepreneurial units throughout the company and to diffuse them rapidly systemwide.

• *Continuous self-renewal.* In most organizations, "continuous learning" means getting better at what we've done in the past. It is really continuous *refinement.* In a rapidly changing world, companies need a process by which they can not just refine the past but reinvent the future; not just drive performance up the learning curve but jump learning curves. CEOs and top executives must be the main drivers of this core process, and to do so effectively they must view the world through the new perspective.

In the old strategy-structure-systems doctrine, most organizational change is by nature architectural. However, at the heart of the new purpose-process-people philosophy of management is a change in the *behavioral* context, what one manager calls the "smell of the place"—the attitude, energy, and commitment that make real change possible. Such change demands more of leaders.

Continuous self-renewal is evident at Kao Company, a Japanese soap and detergent company founded in 1890. When Yoshiro Maruta became president in 1971, he redefined the company not as a soap maker but as an educational institution where each manager's primary responsibility was to teach and to learn every day. Its resulting R&D efforts helped the company expand from household products to paper goods, cosmetics, and even floppy disks—and to become the number one or two competitor in every market it entered.

Moving Beyond Systems to People

The systems in place in most companies share a common characteristic: they are denominated in financial terms—whether return on net assets, sales increase, or profitability. That was one advantage of organizing around yesterday's scarce resource—capital is easily measured. However, with knowledge and expertise the scarce resource, our systems are no longer in line with the real task of management. We now have to stop treating people as an expense line on the income statement, which is what they are considered in a financially driven system, and record them on the balance sheet as true assets. This goes far beyond the banality of "people are our most important assets," as proclaimed in annual reports. This new view of people makes recruitment, development, motivation, engagement, and retention *the* core tasks of any manager.

Taking talent seriously means, for instance, scrapping tight rules about who can approve what kind of capital investments. A division president, for example, may have a $100,000 spending limit; a CEO may need board approval for expenditures above $500,000. Yet in reality, a front-line manufacturing supervisor, a regional sales manager, or a laboratory technician routinely makes $500,000 decisions that are far more important and are absolutely uncontrolled. Those are hiring decisions. The cost of hiring someone, in terms of recruiting, developing, training, and bringing a new employee up to speed—and in terms of the future value that person is expected to create—easily exceeds $500,000 over the tenure of that employee.

Yet how are such crucial decisions made? Say you are an overworked district manager, looking for a salesperson to cover Des Moines. You advertise in the *Des Moines Register* and get a handful of applicants. Assume that all are acceptable but no one stands out; you pick the best of the lot. In effect, you have simply replicated the labor pool, giving the company (at best) no competitive advantage and possibly putting it at a competitive disadvantage. Until you start recruiting as if it were a strategic asset, parity is the best you can hope for. Unless you increase the capability of a work group every time you hire someone you are neglecting your sustainable source of competitive advantage.

The New Role of Leaders

In the emerging post-transformational corporation, the role of all managers has changed dramatically, although management practice often has not. As discussed earlier, the role of front-line managers responsible for business units or sales subsidiaries must evolve from operational implementers to entrepreneurial initiators. Similarly, for senior managers such as those who head up key functions, businesses, or regions, the job has to shift from administrative controller to developmental coach. The primary responsibility must be to develop the people on the front line. How well managers do that is the difference between empowerment and abandonment. True empowerment requires that before responsibility is moved down the organization, those on the front line have the resources, the capability, and the self-discipline to manage their new autonomy. This is the key task of coaching and development.

Senior managers must also play an *organizational* development role. Rather than, as in the past, focusing on pulling up strategic analysis, capital requests, and budget proposals and then sending down strategic plans, capital allocations, and operating budgets, they now must spend more time and energy assembling the teams and task forces to link people and resources across the organization. They must create the channels of communication and forums of cross-unit decision making that foster learning. And they must manage the ongoing tension between long-term and short-term results.

For their part, top-level executives must become sense-makers rather than grand strategists. CEOs rarely have the detailed business and technical knowledge to set anything but the general direction of a complex organization. For instance, after Intel was forced to shift from making memory chips to making microprocessors, CEO Andy Grove found that managers on the front lines had already begun reallocating the resources of the company. "We were fooled by our strategic rhetoric," he said. "But those at the front line could see that we had to retreat from memory chips. . . . People formulate strategy with their fingertips. Our most significant strategic decision was made not in response to some clear-sighted corporate vision but by the marketing and investment decisions of front-line managers who really knew what was going on."

Top-level executives still have to provide a strategic umbrella. But more important, they have to create understanding. Leaders have to shift their balance from managing strategic content to framing organizational and behavioral context, to create a sense of stretch, discipline, trust, and support. Rather than focusing on strategic fit and organizational alignment, they must spend at least as much time trying to create dynamic disequilibrium, challenging the organization's working assumptions, and creating the discomfort that prompts creative action.

How Leaders Create a Sense of Purpose

Percy Barnevik, former CEO of Asea Brown Boveri, created a sense of purpose in a large, complex organization. When Asea merged with Brown Boveri to form ABB in 1988, it took Barnevik only three to six months to clarify the strategy-structure-systems issues. While many urged him to get out of the low growth, low profit power generation and distribution industry, he decided to remain in the business, but to redeploy assets and resources from the mature markets of Europe to North America and the developing markets in Asia and Eastern Europe.

From that point the *strategy* was clear, as was the *structure*. In a world in which organizations have to be both globally efficient and nationally responsive, he created a matrix structure that provided both global and local management. It created the flexibility of small, decentralized units and the market scale of a large, globally integrated corporation. He helped managers learn to manage that tension. One way he did that was to create companywide *systems* that provide clear information, available on-line in real time to every manager. At the core of ABB's systems is ABACUS, the ABB Accounting and *Communication* (not Control) System. The key is to "democratize information" and give operating managers the tools to monitor their own performance. Out of the 35 variables that ABACUS tracks, each manager typically selects for his or her business three or four key performance measures for a given period. Front-line managers compare their results to those reported by other units across the company, and learn from others who are doing better.

In short, the system is used to ensure that managers discipline themselves. And self-discipline is far different from—and much more powerful than—compliance. The system also allowed Barnevik to practice a "fingers in the pie" style of management: If there was a problem he could go down two or three layers and gather his own information—not to micromanage others, but to learn "what's going on, what are you doing about it, and how can I help?"

Barnevik started by defining new strategy. Once those decisions were made, implementing ABB's new structure and systems took about a year. How did Barnevik spend his time the next nine years that he was CEO? He traveled 200 days a year to constantly tell the story of ABB. And that story focused not on strategy, structure, and systems per se, but on the purpose, process, and people that would determine ABB's success.

To be sure, he would talk about being "the dominant power generation equipment company in the world." But he'd go on to talk about bringing power generation to developing countries, cleaning up coal-fired power generation around the world, being the company that brings free market economics to the former Communist countries. He created a sense of pride and purpose in the work of the company.

Great CEOs articulate aspirations that speak to every individual. They know that people want to belong and contribute to an institution that makes a difference.

It is not globalization, information technology, or corporate restructuring that are reshaping the competitive landscape; it is the managerial response to those forces. Entrepreneurial initiative, learning, and self-renewal are rarely achieved through formulaic change, nor through devotion to the managerial models of the past. Companies that have thrived in the new economy—companies like ABB, General Electric, Intel, and Kao—have moved beyond their traditional reliance on strategy, systems, and structure to the new sources of value creation—purpose, process, and people. That move is not a *program;* it is a deep recognition of the new roles and relationships of leaders throughout the enterprise, starting at the top.

Christopher Bartlett is the Daewoo Professor of Business Administration at Harvard Business School. He has worked as a consultant at McKinsey & Company's London office and as a manager for Alcoa and Baxter Laboratories. Bartlett is author or coauthor of more than 40 articles and of six books, including *The Individualized Corporation* and *Managing Across Borders*, both with Sumantra Ghoshal.

11

Building Your
Leadership Brand

Dave Ulrich, Norm Smallwood, and Jack Zenger

---

*Generic models of leadership attributes create little value.
Leadership brand, a competitive advantage, occurs when
leaders at every level of an organization are clear about which
results are most important, develop a consistent approach to
delivering those results, and build attributes that support the
achievement of those results. This succeeds when the right
attributes are linked to strategically desired results. Leadership training, job assignments, 360-degree feedback, and
coaching should focus on both attributes and results.*

Think of leadership as brand. Like product brand, leadership
brand means differentiation that commands a premium
price in the market. Ultimate evidence of leadership brand occurs when a firm's stock market value exceeds that of market or
industry standards. General Electric, for instance, has a market
value $20 billion higher than its breakup value, according to CEO
Jack Welch; much of that can be attributed to the acknowledged
quality and depth of its executive leadership.

Investors perceive that the leaders of such companies have
what it takes to deliver sustained results by managing intangi-
bles such as strategy, organization, and people. Recent research

by Ernst & Young shows that 30 percent to 45 percent of investor decisions may be linked to "quality of management." A leadership brand creates value by differentiating a firm's quality of management.

Leadership as brand brings new meaning to the role and responsibility of leaders. Over the last decade, thousands of studies have attempted to identify how and why leaders succeed. These studies seem to cluster around three factors of leadership: how to *be*, what to *know*, and what to *do*. The first of these focuses on who leaders "are"; these studies underscore the importance of integrity, ambition, concern for others, loyalty, and self-awareness. The second group of studies focuses on what leaders must know to succeed, including how to set direction for their unit (focusing on the future, understanding external events, developing a vision), mobilize individual commitment (building relationships, sharing power and authority, and using emotion), and engender organization capability (leveraging diversity, creating organization systems, using teams). The third set of studies show that leaders need to turn what they *know* into what they *do*. This school of thought focuses on behaviors and actions of leaders, assessing quality of leadership by where, how, and with whom they spend time.

These studies of leadership generally conclude with a list of attributes of successful leaders. Most leadership development efforts today search for a grand set of behavioral characteristics of successful leaders, then create experiences to assist future leaders in developing these characteristics. The leadership industry is full of programs, tools, instruments, and activities based on various models of "leadership competency."

Ironically, although leadership matters more now than ever and although more money is spent seeking the "true" attributes of successful leadership, the quality of leadership seems to be in decline. In many studies leadership tops the list of what is required for firms to succeed in the future. Yet somehow the investment in leadership development does not seem to be having the desired impact. One explanation for this may be that the desired attributes have not been identified clearly or instilled strongly enough within leaders; perhaps more rigorous study of leadership attributes is necessary. We think there are better directions to pursue.

We believe that the concept of leadership brand offers another approach to closing the gap between the investment and impact of leadership.

What's New in Branding

Brands have been identified for years as a way to distinguish and market a product. More recently, brands have been used to build customer commitment to the firm, not just to particular products of the firm. Ask people who frequently shop at Nordstrom, for instance, why they shop there. They will probably cite the service they receive. Ask them for the brand of the merchandise they purchased, and they probably will not be able to tell you. Consumers seldom go to Nordstrom for a particular brand of apparel; they go for the overall experience. Other companies such as Nike and Harley-Davidson have also created firm brand. Nike has created a brand around an understanding of athletes and has branded this understanding across multiple categories—shoes, clothing, sporting equipment, and sporting events. Harley has branded its image of independence, individuality, and freedom across all styles of motorcycles, clothing, and now restaurants.

Similarly, leadership brand lies at the heart of a firm's identity. It occurs when a sufficiently large number of leaders exhibit distinct leadership practices over a number of years. In time the organization creates leaders who are distinct from those of other firms. Focusing exclusively on leadership attributes, however, provides only a generic, not a branded model of leadership. Attributes are necessary but not sufficient for effective leadership.

In a workshop, we asked managers to list the leadership characteristics desired by their firms. These managers, from diverse industries and with different strategies, all described nearly identical requirements—act with integrity, set a vision, have energy, execute strategy, and energize others. It would have been impossible to match the companies with the leadership competencies they presented. These attributes have become generic. And like generic products, generic models of leadership create little value. Investing more effort defining and developing these behavior-based attributes will not increase leadership impact. Impact comes when leaders are branded.

A Formula for Leadership

Leadership brand occurs when leaders at every level are clear about which results are most important, develop a consistent approach to delivering these results, and build attributes that support the achievement of those results. Firms admired for their high quality of management in the annual *Fortune* survey have created distinct leadership brands. General Electric leaders are known for their ability to deliver financial results by working hard and engaging their employees. Coca-Cola leaders have traditionally increased shareholder value and built brand loyalty through their ability to learn, distribute products, and compete globally. Dell Computer leaders have a reputation for achieving results through innovative distribution and customer service. Southwest Airlines leaders create and live in a culture of enthusiasm and fun, yet dedicated to efficient service and financial results. Intel leaders identify and respond to sudden market shifts and encourage strategic debate. Disney leaders commit to delivering families a positive and unique experience by hiring, motivating, and communicating with employees.

In each of these cases, highly admired firms are imbued with their own brand of leaders. Their brands succeed when the right attributes are linked to desired results, as represented in a simple formula: *branded leadership = attributes = results*.

Leaders who score high on attributes but low on results do not truly lead. These leaders may do good works, relate well to others, and act with honor and integrity. However, if they fail to deliver desired results they cannot be effective. Kay Whitmore, former CEO of Eastman Kodak, is widely recognized for his unimpeachable character and integrity while he led Kodak. But most will not remember him as a great leader. On his watch, Kodak faced increasing competitive pressures that required a transformation of the business. Whitmore was unable to grow the company fast enough to stay ahead of competitors. He resisted those who urged him to cut costs through layoffs until a new strategy took hold. The board lost patience and eventually replaced him.

Leadership is more than image. All the integrity, energy, and goodwill in the world will not hide poor performance. Without clear and visible results, leadership never endures. Leaders strong in attributes alone may have mastered the language of leadership, but not the essence.

Conversely, leaders who achieve results but lack integrity, character, and values face a different challenge: winning the support necessary for long-term performance. They often take or receive credit for results they did not produce, so they have difficulty replicating or extending those results. They do not have the trust and goodwill of constituents. They find it difficult to focus attention on new initiatives or strategies. These leaders seldom create a long-term legacy, because their results were not sustainable by their behaviors. Al Dunlap, former CEO of Scott Paper and Sunbeam, achieved results without positive attributes. He dazzled investors with his focus on cost cutting, layoffs, and other short-term turnaround techniques. Employees, their families, and communities watched "Chainsaw Al" fly high with a mixture of awe, anger, and resentment. When Sunbeam stumbled and Dunlap was ousted, many cheered. His short-term, numbers-only results combined with what many considered an uncaring approach made him a short-time wonder. Highly effective leaders get results and get them in a way that demonstrates high character.

When we speak about the importance of leaders' producing results, we often receive a resounding, "Duh . . . of course, leaders must produce results." In the business world, especially, performance is paramount, as frequently evidenced by CEO firings. However, most organizations' leadership development efforts focus almost exclusively on building attributes. Attaining results is an assumed, not explicit, expectation. Leadership investment falls short when it focuses on either attributes *or* results; it succeeds when it delivers both attributes *and* results.

Creating a Leadership Brand

Branded leaders use desired attributes to produce desired outcomes. Sometimes leaders start with the attributes they have developed and apply them to get results; at other times, they start by clarifying the results that must be accomplished through their leadership attributes. By linking the attributes that are appropriate to the organization and the results that best serve its purpose, leaders create a brand that distinguishes them from leaders elsewhere. This is a four-step process with the first two steps interchangeable.

Step 1: Specify Desired Results

Desired results are strategically balanced and measurable. Desired results also must serve multiple constituents. Robert Kaplan and David Norton, professors at Harvard Business School and respected consultants, draw on stakeholder theory of organizations to create what they call a "balanced scorecard." We have adapted their work to suggest that leaders' results be balanced across four groups of stakeholders: employees, the organization, customers, and investors. Leaders who excel in only one area are not effective. Achieving workforce results, demonstrated by high levels of employee commitment and skills, means little if employees' efforts fail to satisfy customers. In such cases, the leader has failed the balance test. Leaders face a difficult challenge in trying to balance and attain results in all four stakeholder areas. Results-based leaders may, at times, make the deliberate choice of emphasizing one dimension over another, but they cannot afford to ignore any of them for long.

In addition to balance, leadership results must be measured. From a list of possible indicators, a leader may create a dashboard that reflects his or her unique business requirements (see table). Once desired outcomes are selected, this dashboard may then be monitored to assess leadership results.

Step 2: Identify Desired Attributes

Defining desired attributes (who leaders need to be, what they need to know, and what they need to do) is practiced by many organizations using well-crafted models of leadership. Successful attribute-based models are characterized by three factors.

First, attributes must focus on *future* leadership behavior. Some leadership-attribute models identify high-performing leaders and those doing moderately well, then do critical incident analysis to

Branded leaders identify the results they're expected to deliver and closely monitor their performance in meeting those results. This table shows examples of results important to each of four stakeholders—employees, customers, the organization, and investors—along with "vital signs" of progress.

Employee Vital Signs	
Desired Result	**Indicators**
Workforce competence	Percentage of key positions for which backup talent is available
	Extent to which the company's vision is shared among all employees
Commitment	Retention and turnover (voluntary versus involuntary; low versus high performers)
	Employee satisfaction or commitment index
	Productivity

Organization Vital Signs	
Desired Result	**Indicators**
Organizational learning	Resources (money and time) spent on learning forums for technology transfers
	Percent of revenues from new products
Speed	Product time to breakeven
	Cycle time for new products
Accountability	Quality (against world-class standards) of products and services
	Removal of poor performers

Measuring Your Vital Signs

Customer Vital Signs	
Desired Result	**Indicators**
Customization	Assessed delivery of value proposition for target customers
	Comparative performance of products or services vis-à-vis competitor
Customer intimacy	Survey data of customer commitment
	Share of key customers' spending

Investor Vital Signs	
Desired Result	**Indicators**
Growth	Growth by product, geography, channel, customer, and total revenue
Cost control	Reduced cost of transaction work (for example, payroll, accounts receivable)
	History of staying on budget at every level
Management equity	Comments and perceptions of analysts and opinion makers
	Executives' personal financial stake in the firm

Measuring Your Vital Signs *(continued)*

determine what knowledge or behavior separates the two. This is dangerous, because even when done well, these models may identify what successful leaders *did*, not what they will need to do. More effective models require an understanding of future strategy that can be articulated in behavioral terms.

Second, attribute-based models must win the support of line managers. The task of creating these models often falls solely to human resource managers or external consultants. However, leaders, line managers, and employees usually commit more to models that bear the stamp of authentic experience, not just valid research. Heavily involving line managers in crafting attribute models increases their commitment to them.

Third, attribute models must be put into practice. Sometimes more resources are spent creating models than using them. To be widely used, models must focus on the critical few attributes of successful leaders. They must be relevant across all levels of the organization. Effective attribute models must be woven into all management decisions, including hiring, training, development, promotion, career management, compensation, and communication.

When done well, attribute models help leaders. They assure that leaders have the character, knowledge, and practices that are important to a firm and that they can and will take the appropriate actions. But unless they link all this to results, they fall short of a leadership brand.

Step 3: Link Attributes to Results

Attributes may be tied to results by completing the phrase "so that" for each attribute. For example, instead of having a goal "to implement total quality management in operations," a more results-oriented leader wants "to implement total quality management in operations *so that* our quality is not more than 25 defects per 1,000." The power of this approach is evident in many such statements that link leadership attributes to the vital signs of results. For example, *Leaders in my organization must . . .*

- Create a vision for e-commerce *so that* we identify and invest in new distribution channels that grow revenues 15 percent in the next year without cannibalizing revenues from existing channels.

- Build collaborative relationships *so that* talented employees feel more committed to their work team as measured by their retention and by an employee commitment index.

- Exhibit energy and personal presence *so that* investors endorse the management team as measured by shareholder value above financial expectations in our industry.

If a leader begins by defining desired results, then those results need to be linked to appropriate attributes. Otherwise, the results may be isolated, one-time events. To tie results to appropriate attributes, leaders should complete the phrase "because of" for each goal. This assures that leaders have the means by which to accomplish their results. For example, *Leaders in my organization must . . .*

- Increase revenue from targeted customers *because of* our ability to understand customer buying criteria.

- Retain the best and brightest employees *because of* efforts to involve employees in key decisions that affect the company.

- Be more innovative as measured by percentage of revenue from new products *because of* our ability to move ideas across organizational boundaries.

Unless leaders understand both what is expected of them (their results) and how they are expected to achieve them (their leadership attributes) they cannot distinguish their own or their organization's brand of leadership.

Step 4: Invest in Results-Based Leadership Development

Once a leadership brand has been crafted with both attributes and results, leadership development activities may be created to further the leadership brand. Leadership development investments may be woven together to form a coherent leadership strategy.

When investments in training, job assignments, 360-degree feedback, coaching, mentoring, and technology-based learning focus on both attributes and results, leadership development creates more impact. For example, Southern Company, a global electric utility, created a leadership development experience focused on results. This training helped leaders identify and deliver results in such areas as service quality, safety, cost management, and community relations. By focusing the development on results, the participants in the development experience become more aware of the unique, or branded, leadership within the Southern Company.

Benefits of Leadership Brand

Any good leader wants to be a better one. Leaders who want to be better need to understand the outcomes they must produce for their organization. This requires understanding of strategy and how they contribute to it. It also requires that their knowledge and behaviors support the strategic goals. With branded leadership, everyone gains a line of sight to what is really desired. When an entire leadership team focuses on delivering the same results and has developed relevant attributes to deliver these results, they gain a competitive advantage.

Organizations that succeed do so with successful leadership. Branded leadership creates a distinct culture that permeates the enterprise. Employees know what is expected of them, both in terms of how they work and what they must accomplish at work. Customers receive a more consistent value proposition—whether it is better service, higher quality or performance, lower prices, or greater levels of innovation. Investors have confidence in the quality of leadership within the firm and offer a market value premium in response.

By building branded leaders, our business, social, and public institutions may begin to close the gap between the substantial investment already made in leadership and the growing need for ever more effective leaders in the future.

Dave Ulrich is professor of business administration at the University of Michigan and codirects Michigan's Human Resource Executive Program. He is editor of *Human Resource Management Journal* and has been named by *BusinessWeek* as one of the world's top 10 management educators. He is coauthor of several books, including *Results-Based Leadership* with Jack Zenger and Norm Smallwood.

Norm Smallwood leads Provant's Results-Based Leadership Company. He was a founding partner of Novations Group, a change management consulting firm. Previously he worked at

Procter & Gamble and Esso Resources Canada. He has written for leading business and technical journals on topics ranging from business strategy to individual performance and development.

Jack Zenger is vice chairman and director of Provant, the world's largest performance-improvement service company. Previously he was chairman of the Times Mirror Training Group and was cofounder and CEO of Zenger-Miller, a leading management development firm. He has taught at University of Southern California and Stanford University and is author of five books.

12

Why Vision Matters

Robert Knowling

Knowling argues that vision and values shape organizational behavior and spark strategic action. He presents steps for defining, articulating, and propagating vision and values: (1) assessing the organization, industry, and economic sector; (2) talking to new employees; (3) matching attributes and effort to results; (4) connecting with customers, partners, and front-line employees; and (5) leading for change. In addition, he presents five warning signs of conditions that can undermine change.

In business, as in life, good intentions are often lost. Our everyday practices, not our espoused values, define who we are. To align good intentions with effective practice, leaders need to define a vision, articulate values, and infuse both into every aspect of the business.

Most leaders love to make strategy, but it is vision and values that spawn strategic action. The absence of a vision will doom any strategy—especially a strategy for change. A true vision shapes your hiring, assessment, and promotion of employees, and your behavior toward customers, partners, and investors. It is a more powerful tool for leading an organization than any market analysis or spreadsheet. But defining your vision (the expression of what your company wants to be) and articulating your values (the principles governing how you operate) are not easy or painless.

The first step in visioning is to assess your organization, your industry, and your sector of the economy. What do you do uncommonly well, and how do you fit into the changing landscape? For me, the next step is to take the management team to an offsite to look in depth at these questions (see "An Exercise in Visioning").

In addition, every new employee in our company goes through a three-day visions and values process within 90 days. I talk to every hire about who we are as a company. One of the values we discuss is having integrity in every business transaction. That's not an earthshaking aspiration, but we give it some bite. We talk about how we deal with each other. Honesty is the order of the day, in everything from how we present reports to how we book sales. It's all-encompassing and uncompromising—and we've been tested on it. We once had to dismiss a highly visible manager for a violation of our values. It would have been easy to look the other way. But, as GE's Jack Welch used to say, you must be public about the consequences of breaching core values. When you announce simply that an executive has "left to pursue other business interests," you lose the chance to make a statement about values.

Matching Effort to Results

Many people in the company wonder why we invest such time and effort inculcating our vision and values. We will be a negative-cash-flow business for the next two and a half years; why are vision and values a priority? Why not invest in marketing or delivery systems? Leaders are always tempted to focus

An Exercise in Visioning

How can a management team build a shared vision and translate that vision into a strategy? I have used a process in three different organizations that has helped develop both a vision and a plan for the future.

First we listen to Martin Luther King Jr.'s "I Have a Dream" speech. We talk about one leader at a point in history and note that his speech said nothing about the current state of affairs. Instead it painted a picture of the future. It tapped a deep aspiration.

We try to define our own aspirations for the organization. Then we each imagine that *Fortune* or *BusinessWeek* is writing about our company five years from now. We have just achieved our dream, and the reporter asks exactly how we did it. The combination of thinking aspirationally about where you want to be and then tactically about how you would get there helps crystallize a vision for the enterprise.

That process led us to see we wanted to be "the next great admired company"—a company that delights customers, attracts top talent, rewards investors, challenges an industry, serves the community. Our strategies may change, but those aspirations do not.

Had King lived, he would have witnessed an extraordinary phenomenon—the achievement of a far-reaching vision articulated at a time when the leader had no idea how to get there. That is the challenge of leadership.

on core business deliverables rather than "the distraction" of vision and values. But leaders have to pay attention to both. I invest our resources in vision and values because company culture is inseparable from strategy—and because I don't want to wake up one day with a profitable organization that does not have a soul. Without an identity that we purposefully shape, we have no future.

A disciplined approach to vision and values helps employees understand what's important in the business. It tells us not just what, but also how and why we are expected to deliver. We assess people according to two criteria—their current performance and their values. We use a nine-cell matrix developed by Action Learning Associates (see figure) in our hiring process, performance reviews, and succession planning.

For instance, in succession planning, I first rate each manager's performance and leadership values. Then the rest of the management team challenges me based on their observations. Rarely do we agree on all candidates, but they usually fall into one of three groups. There are the easy calls—high performers with good values. There are others who have the right attitudes but have performance problems. We try to help them succeed if we can. Finally come those who get results, but do so at the

People rated low in leadership and values—even if rated high for performance—have a risky future.

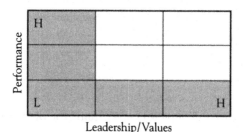

Managing for Values
   Source: Noel Tichy and Eli Cohen, *The Leadership Engine: How Winning Companies Build Leaders at All Levels,* HarperCollins, 1997, p. 263.

expense of teamwork, integrity, openness to change, development of others, or the interests of customers. People who don't
share our values are cancerous to the organization, regardless of
their performance. In my experience, every time you invest trying to save these people you end up regretting it. It's simply too
difficult to change people's values.

Putting Teeth into HR

Obviously, it is not enough to cheerlead for values; you still have
to make tough business decisions. In 1998 I joined Covad Communications, the first company other than a traditional phone
company to offer Digital Subscriber Lines for high-speed Internet access. After less than 30 days on the job, I saw that our sales
strategy was wrong. We would never get the necessary reach or
volume with a direct sales force; we needed multiple channels
and partners. About 40 people, in a company of less than 200 at
the time, were affected by this change. My opening act was to
say that 20 percent of the workforce had the wrong skills for the
job, and by the way, the company's current strategy was doomed.

The only way a leader wins support for those kinds of decisions is to make the business case, to respect people and the organization, and to slowly build trust. No boss can do that without
strong leadership in the management team and throughout the
organization.

We build trust, and develop other leaders, by talking honestly.
Every other month our senior team takes one or two days to examine our strategy, our effectiveness as a team, and own growth
as leaders. These are difficult sessions. We try to get as brutally
honest as we can with each other. There is nothing I like about
those sessions. I put myself front and center to get facilitated

feedback on how I'm doing as a leader—what works, what doesn't work. This opens lines of communication; it discourages political agendas. Eventually it brings clarity about the way we operate. We gain rich perspective on our business and ourselves because we are a diverse team in every sense—thought leadership, culture, religion, race, gender.

Walking the Line

Leaders also must connect with customers, partners, and frontline employees. If you really want to understand a problem, go to the front line and give people your ear. It is amazing what you will find out about your business, your customers, and how life really is.

I recently made changes in our business as a result of a visit to a reseller of our service. My host wanted to give me an executive tour, but I asked if I could sit with someone who worked on our account. It was a revelation. The young woman I met showed me what she had to go through to do business with us. She was trying to correct a mistake on a customer order. She had to talk to four people at Covad—and *none* of them could fix the problem. Why not? That order passed through our company like a part on an assembly line. No one had accountability for where it went next. It reminded me of a culture I know well—the phone company. Of course, phone company mentality is not unique to the phone company.

We implemented a system that I think will change the way our partners view us. We made a supervisor and a dedicated team responsible for each of our channel partners. It will create a new customer experience. But I never would have seen that problem if I did not sit with someone who does our work.

It takes time and commitment to be at the front line. It also takes an ability to relate to people. One of the first things I learned as a manager was a communication technique called FORM. You can learn a lot about people and open useful conversations about your business by asking about any of these elements:

Family—what's happening with spouse, children, immediate relatives (usually the most important thing in people's lives)

Occupation—what they like or don't like about their job

Recreation—how they spend their time away from the job

Money—how they spend it, what they enjoy, what's important to them

I use these experiences to show other leaders in the business how important it is to get out and to touch the people, feel the people. Leaders lead through stories. They use stories as tools for engagement, for change, for honesty, and for values.

Leading for Change

Leadership is about managing the constant of change. The market and the world shaping your market are never going to stand still—especially in the New Economy. One technical breakthrough or blockbuster deal could render your strategy irrelevant overnight. Leaders have no choice but to be fluid, to learn to deal with the ambiguity, to be able to change their business model. That is why it is so important to have an overarching vision and values to guide you.

But, given a clear vision and strong values, how do we help move an organization forward? I have discovered few great ideas on my own; friends, colleagues, and mentors have taught me most of what I know. However, I have led large-scale change efforts in three organizations, and have found that several principles hold.

Start with the Answers

The boss does not have all the answers—no one does. When a team is floundering, you need somebody to step up and say, "I've got an answer." It doesn't even have to be the *right* answer. If you bring everybody into the process, you may discover quickly that it's *not* the right answer. What's important is to spark action, debate, and a sense of urgency.

Set Bold Goals

A bold goal gets everyone's attention, and it provides a simple measure of success for everyone in the company. Last year, for instance, we set a goal to extend our network to 40 percent of homes and 45 percent of businesses in the United States by the end of 2000. This is not about setting goals so high that people simply give their best or burn out trying. Most systems can quickly realize 20 percent or even 40 percent gains in efficiency once you target a problem. That's been my experience every place I've worked.

Supply Resources

One of the things leaders can provide that others probably cannot is a commitment of the organization's time, money, people, or training. My job is to allocate resources, and to do that effectively I have to listen, recognize, and celebrate success.

Coach the Team

I understand the value of a team. When a team clicks it becomes far more than the sum of its parts; the opposite is also true. Great coaches, and effective leaders, understand everybody's strength and everybody's weakness. They know how to play to those strengths. Your job as a leader is to lift the game of the others on the team. I hold leaders accountable for that.

Know the Business and How You Make a Difference

A lot of people don't understand the business they're in or the value proposition they offer. As a business leader you have to be sure that everybody understands how you make money (or, in the public or nonprofit sector, how you get cost-effective results). You have to break down the top line results so that people throughout the enterprise understand how they contribute. At U.S. West I was able to show the line installers why they each needed to make six installations a day to support the larger business. People have to be able to go home every day and know if they made a difference.

Understand the Human Connection

Never forget or forsake the people who are affected by your decisions, and who in turn affect your ability to implement decisions. You cannot be sentimental in shaping the right strategy for the future. Nor can you bully, badger, or fail to respect people. I've never seen transformational efforts succeed when leaders showed no concern for others. There is a humane way to deal with people even when you have to deliver tough news.

Never Compromise on Performance

In the phone company, at least until recently, no one's job was ever at risk. If you had a problem employee, you moved that employee into another department. It was demoralizing for the high performers, degrading to the poor performers, and toxic to any change effort. Yet most poor performers know they're poor performers. If you've been honest in your assessments of them and treated them fairly and respectfully, they can usually accept the fact that they have not made the grade.

Knowing the Warning Signs

Most change efforts fall far short of their potential. Even with principled leadership, implementing change is a messy, perplexing, and never-ending process. I have found five warning signs that can undermine change.

Underestimating the Culture

We all have our own image of bureaucracy: the Phone Company. The Government. The School System. But bureaucracy is above all a mentality. Many of the syndromes of the 30,000-member organization are replicated in the 100-member enterprise. Every organization has a culture—sometimes two or three fighting for control. The culture determines how people work together and how they respond to change. No leader can succeed without understanding and shaping the norms at work.

Declaring Victory

Most of the time when you start change initiatives, you get immediate lift. The easy pickings are always the first to harvest.

It's important to show early results and to celebrate success. But if you don't work for systematic, continuous improvement, the organization will snap back to original shape. True victory is like a compelling vision—it is never really achieved.

Letting People Catch Their Breath

As you reach certain milestones you want to take the pressure off—to slow down, let people rest. You cannot. Change has to be part of everyone's job description. You cannot keep people in perpetual fire-fighting mode, but initially, people *do* have to respond as if their house were on fire. You then have to create a structure and ongoing process to make change a part of the business.

Delegating the Change Process

The senior executive has to walk the halls, make the calls, be physically and emotionally present. You cannot tell subordinates to present your plan to the staff and give you a weekly update (a popular approach in Silicon Valley). I have found that people love to give PowerPoint presentations, but they hate to actually give you information. The change process starts with you—how you run your meetings, manage your calendar, share information.

Believing Your Own Press Clips

It is easy to be seduced by success. Every leader receives glowing reports from the field. Discount the good news and pay attention to your doubts. Both personal and organizational success are fragile and fleeting. You should take pride in your and your team's accomplishments, but you have to let people know that the best is always ahead of you.

Leaving a Legacy

You cannot build value for customers, shareholders, or the community without a vision and values for your organization. You build value by becoming the leader in your field, the company that everybody wants to work for, buy from, or invest in.

It takes tremendous confidence to stake out that territory and to lead others toward it. You have to withstand the doubts and loneliness of leadership. At the same time you have to acknowledge to yourself and others that you don't always know how you will reach your destination. For others to follow you through times of uncertainty requires mutual trust and faith. That is what clarity of vision and commitment to values can bring.

I once thought that the test of personal leadership was the number of people that follow a leader when he or she moves to a new organization. But what is more rewarding is to look across an organization and see the number of leaders in place, people who share a common aspiration and have the tools and wisdom—the vision and values—to achieve something great. That is any leader's greatest legacy.

Robert Knowling is chairman and CEO of Internet Access Technologies. Previously he was chairman and CEO of Covad Communications, and he led large-scale change efforts at U.S. West and at Ameritech. Knowling has been featured in *Fast Company, Forbes, BusinessWeek,* and *The Industry Standard.*

Index

Leader to Leader

A *quarterly publication of*
the Drucker Foundation
and Jossey-Bass Publishers
Frances Hesselbein,
Editor-in-Chief

Leader to Leader is a unique management publication, a quarterly report on management, leadership, and strategy written by today's top leaders *themselves*. Four times a year, *Leader to Leader* keeps you ahead of the curve by bringing you the latest offerings from a peerless selection of world-class executives, best-selling management authors, leading consultants, and respected social thinkers, making *Leader to Leader* unlike any other magazine or professional publication today.

Think of it as a short, intensive seminar with today's top thinkers and doers—people like Peter F. Drucker, Rosabeth Moss Kanter, Max De Pree, Charles Handy, Esther Dyson, Stephen Covey, Meg Wheatley, Peter Senge, and others.

Subscriptions to **Leader to Leader** are $199.00.
501(c)(3) nonprofit organizations can subscribe for $99.00 (must supply tax-exempt ID number when subscribing). Prices subject to change without notice.

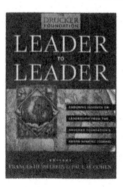

Leader to Leader

Enduring Insights on Leadership from the
Drucker Foundation's Award-Winning Journal
Frances Hesselbein, Paul M. Cohen, Editors

The world's thought leaders come together in *Leader to Leader*, an inspiring examination of mission, leadership, values, innovation, building collaborations, shaping effective institutions, and creating community. Management pioneer Peter F. Drucker; Southwest Airlines CEO Herb Kelleher; best-selling authors Warren Bennis, Stephen R. Covey, and Charles Handy; Pulitzer Prize winner Doris Kearns Goodwin; Harvard professors Rosabeth Moss Kanter and Regina Herzlinger; and learning organization expert Peter Senge are among those who share their knowledge and experience in this essential resource. Their essays will spark ideas, open doors, and inspire all those who face the challenge of leading in an ever-changing environment.

For a reader's guide, see www.leaderbooks.org

Hardcover   ISBN 0-7879-4726-1 $27.00

FAX	**CALL**	**MAIL**	**WEB**
Toll Free	Toll Free	Jossey-Bass Publishers	Secure ordering at:
24 hours a day:	6am to 5pm PST:	989 Market St.	www.josseybass.com
800-605-2665	800-956-7739	San Francisco, CA 94105-1741